14

Property Investment Depreciation and Obsolescence

Property Investment Depreciation and Obsolescence

Andrew Baum

London

First published 1991
by Routledge
11 New Fetter Lane, London EC4P 4EE

© 1991 Andrew Baum

Printed and bound in Great Britain by Mackays of Chatham PLC, Kent

British Library Cataloguing in Publication Data

Baum, Andrew *1953–*
    Property investment depreciation and obsolescence.
    1. Great Britain. Real property. Investment
    I. Title
    332.63240941

    ISBN 0-415-04802-8

Contents

Part three
Models and Conclusions

Preface

The 1980's was a decade which saw property research come of age as an applied discipline which contributed to decision-making. Struggling to break free from the bonds imposed by the need for mind-numbing promotional material, property researchers formed themselves into a society, property investors themselves took on whole teams of researchers to guide the management of property portfolios; and property developers increasingly turned to specialist boutiques for advice.

Property indices proliferated, but serious attempts at establishing measures of market performance were made, and comprehensive property databanks became established. Property itself became respectable as an asset class as a result of the efforts of the urban geographers, planners and statisticians who turned themselves into property researchers and data gatherers.

Indeed, the 1980's was the decade of the applied urban geographer turned property researcher. Understanding the spatial nature of property as an investment and the demographics which underpin the demand for it, many a potential town planner was transformed into a property research entrepreneur, or (even more surprising) the research partner in a firm of chartered surveyors.

The 1990's, on the other hand, will be the decade of quantitative property economists. Forecasts of property values will be published. The basic theory of the management of portfolios of assets will begin to be applied to property and put widely into practice. Attention will turn from soft property research to the interpretation of the hard data that is now available for analysis.

Investors will require a model which tells them whether property, and sub-sectors of the property market, are cheap or dear. They will need to understand the forces which drive yields up and down. They will need forecasts of rental change. They will have to develop a feel for the appropriate risk premium over a risk-free opportunity cost for particular property types. And they will need to measure depreciation.

This book is an attempt to suggest a means of measuring, and taking account of, depreciation and obsolescence. It is hoped that it will help us progress a little in the early 1990's. It would also be pleasing if others involved in the property development and construction industries derived some insight from it. Most of all, I hope that property researchers are doing so well in their new careers that they can afford to buy it.

Andrew Baum
Oxfordshire

Figures

Tables

Equations

Acknowledgements

Ian Sibley acted as research assistant in the project which significantly contributed to these contents. He organised and reported the industrial study described in Chapter 7 and contributed many valuable ideas, especially useful in establishing the classification model described in Chapter 4. I am grateful for his efforts over the period of the project. I would also like to thank Gerald Brown for his technical advice.

Hill Samuel and Richard Ellis provided financial and intellectual support for the project referred to above. In particular I would like to thank Brian Wootton of Hill Samuel, and John Sloan, Iain Reid, Gillian Eleftheriou, Colin Barber, Mike Warner and Alan Froggatt at Richard Ellis for their help in forming some of the ideas which are developed in this book. The hard work of Mark McAlister, Roger Lister, Colin Bell, Rodney Powell, Lesley Morley, Mike Daggett, Tim Roberton and Julian Nairn at Richard Ellis contributed invaluable data.

Professor Alan Evans and Peter Byrne of the University of Reading provided careful and sensitive advice in difficult circumstances.

The Property Research Team at Prudential Portfolio Managers Ltd provided an inspiration, a team spirit which is unrepeatable, and a degree of support which exceeded reasonable expectations on several occasions. Bryan MacGregor, Paul McNamara, George Matysiak and Andy Schofield all contributed greatly to my education. Jacqueline Donovan is responsible for the quality of presentation of this book and I cannot thank her enough.

Chapter 1

Introduction: property investment analysis in its context

1. Property as an investment

In 1977 the index value of the average prime (institutional quality) office in the UK stood at 100 (Investors Chronicle Hillier Parker Market Indicators). By 1985 the index had risen to 208. The average prime office increased in value by 108% over that 8-year period, an average annual increase of 9.6%.

In 1975 a major UK pension fund bought a 10-year old office block in North London for £2.825m. In 1977 the building had increased in value by 23.9% (or 11.3% per annum) and was valued at £3.5m. It was 10 years old, and showing some signs of age. Nonetheless, it was performing quite well in a relatively quiet market.

By 1985, eight years later, the building was valued at only £3.2m. Had it kept pace with the index, its value would have been £7.28m. Instead, it had fallen in value by 8.6%, or 1% per annum, and as a result was now worth only 44% of the index value for average prime offices in the UK.

The building was now 18 years old. The relative attractiveness of the location had not changed very much, but 1960's office buildings had become highly unpopular within a very weak market for office investments, and in addition this building had developed structural problems which were not evident at the time. The property had suffered severe depreciation.

The subject of this book is the analysis of property investment depreciation and obsolescence. Analysis in this context means "the estimation of the worth of a property investment to an investor" (Baum and Crosby, 1988), where:

> ...worth may be expressed in three forms. Where the price of an investment is known, for example in a retrospective analysis after a sale, or where negotiations for a purchase by private treaty have neared completion, then the worth of the investment must be expressed either as a *rate of return* or as an excess value over the price (*net present value*) at a given target rate. Where the price is unknown, for example where an investment is to be sold by auction, the analysis is aimed at an assessment of the *capital value* of the investment, or the maximum price that can be paid, given a target rate of return.

The subject matter of the research described in this book is focussed on one particular variable, depreciation, for two reasons: firstly, because it is concerned with worth, and secondly because little is known about it. The twin aims of this work are to gain a fuller understanding of the way in which property investments depreciate and to be able to use that information to analyse property investments.

Investment is "a vehicle into which funds can be placed with the expectation that they will be preserved or increase in value and/or generate positive returns" (Gitman and Joehnk, 1984); it is also described as "the sacrifice of something now for the prospect of later benefits" (Greer and Farrell, 1984).

The generation of returns and benefits can arise in three ways. These are:

i generating a flow of income, or reducing income tax;

ii generating a return of capital, whether it be less than, equal to or more than the initial sacrifice, or reducing capital tax; or

iii producing a psychic income, a positive feeling induced by ownership of an investment which may be incapable of financial quantification.

Investment return is therefore a function of income, capital return and psychic income. Property is now examined in that light.

2. The qualities of property

The income produced by a property investment is in the form of rent reduced by operating expenses of various types. While operating expenses will be incurred both regularly (for example, management and the provision of services) and infrequently (for example, repairs), rent will normally be received at regular intervals, quarterly in advance being typical in the UK. In a period of inflation, a freehold property investment may be expected to show a profit upon resale so that capital return is usually in the form of a gain. Finally, a psychic income will often be induced by property ownership.

Consequently, the return from property is generated as follows. Firstly, the investment may produce a return of capital by resale which may differ in amount from the original investment. In freehold investments, there is an effective limit (land value) to any loss; in leaseholds, a decline to nil value must eventually be suffered. Secondly, the investment provides a varying income depending upon rental values, themselves a product of the demand for use of the property and the supply of alternatives. Variance of the income is reduced by leases and long review periods, and upward-only reviews will ensure, at worst, a level income. Finally, there may be a very high psychic income produced by property investment, associated with pride of ownership of a tangible, visible asset, rights of occupation, relationships with tenants, the opportunity for active management and benefits such as building naming rights.

Institutions dominate the UK property market (McIntosh and Sykes, 1985), and most institutional investment funds are currently exposed to conventional gilts and other fixed interest securities, equities, index-linked gilts, property and cash. Property has therefore to be dealt with in the context of these investment types. In detail, factors relevant to a consideration of the relative attractions of property against these alternatives are income and capital growth, psychic income, operating expenses, liquidity, tax efficiency and risk.

Income and capital growth

The current income level may not be a good indicator of future income levels. Consequently, the initial yield may not indicate the continuing income yield that will be produced by an investment over its holding period. Where that yield is expected to increase, the initial yield may be low, indicative of a higher price being paid.

Fixed interest gilts produce a fixed income and the price reflects that fact. There is no prospect of income growth or, conversely, of monetary income loss. The initial yield is a perfect indication of the continuing income yield (*running yield*). Index-linked gilts, on the other hand, produce an index-linked income. As long as inflation is expected to be positive, income growth may be anticipated and the initial yield should therefore be lower, *ceteris paribus*, than for fixed interest gilts.

Ordinary shares produce dividends which depend upon (a) profits and (b) the management's dividend and reinvestment strategy. The latter is often used to smooth away variations in the former, so that a broad relationship between inflation and dividends may be theorised via profit levels, and in an inflationary era where production grows in line and the company's profit share is not eroded, the profits of an average company might be expected to increase (see Fraser, 1984).

For property, a similar relationship between *inflation* and rents may be discernible. The Investors Chronicle Hillier Parker Rent Index (May 1985) shows that over the period 1977 to 1985 inflation was accurately matched, on average, by rental values (see Table 1).

Table 1: Rent indices adjusted for inflation, 1965 - 1985

Year	ICHP Rent Index	Shops	Offices	Industrials
1965	87	87	86	86
1969	106	102	113	98
1972	121	123	131	101
1974	155	142	188	114
1975	155	140	180	127
1976	112	110	115	107
1977	**100**	**100**	**100**	**100**
1978	103	109	101	101
1979	112	123	106	110
1980	107	117	100	108
1981	105	112	101	101
1982	102	110	100	96
1983	101	111	99	93
1984	101	113	98	91
1985	101	119	97	88

Source: Investors Chronicle Hillier Parker Rent Index

Causes of income growth other than inflation may also be considered. There may be prospects for *real growth* so that particular sectors of the market, defined by type or region, may perform particularly well over a particular period (see, for example, offices over the period 1969 to 1974, in Table 1).

One of the major problems of this type of analysis is the quality of the data. There are no definitive rental value indices; and it was not until the mid 1960's that *any* indices of rental value movements were published. A recent study (Crosby, 1985) attempted to remedy this at the local level by constructing a shop rental value index for Nottingham city centre for 1910 to 1981. The results from 1910 to 1960 are set out in Table 2 and show that between 1910 and 1960 a real growth rate of 1.25% per annum was achieved. Theorising simplistically, a supply artificially restricted by planning controls may be set against increasing demand as behaviour patterns change and population increases to cause real rental growth. A similar effect may be translated into real dividend increases for ordinary shares; it is not present for fixed interest (conventional) gilts.

There may also be *monopoly profits* which accrue to property owners. Property interests are unique. Although the impact of heterogeneity will vary according to circumstances, extra gains may be made by exploiting the resulting monopoly position. An extreme example of this is marriage value. The owner of a mid-length leasehold interest will almost certainly be unable to sell to an investor at a price which matches the gain which the freehold reversioner could make by its surrender. Monopoly profits may as a result accrue to both freeholder and leaseholder. Other *special purchasers* (funds which are especially keen to buy a property for portfolio balance, for example) may appear.

Re-zoning or betterment created for example by the siting of a new motorway or by the reallocation of land planned for commercial development may well produce capital gains in excess of inflation. These can also be termed monopoly profits, because they may be the product of the exploitation of monopolistic information or of monopolistic land ownership.

Finally, *gearing* or leverage, the use of borrowed funds to exaggerate capital and income growth, is particularly suited to property investment which is regarded as excellent collateral security. Such gains can be maximised by increasing the gearing level in times of high price increases, especially if interest rates are low and taxation rules are favourable. The risk of financial failure resulting from interest rate increases or falling prices is at the same time increased by such a policy.

Nonetheless, the general inflationary trend since the second world war and the particular experience of 1960-1972, when many massive gains resulted from such policies (see Marriott, 1967 and Rose, 1985), provides an example of a sustained period which demonstrated the benefits of gearing. While equities may also be geared (for example by the use of options), property is perfectly placed to benefit from the advantages of leverage, especially when downside risk may be controlled by the use of upward-only rent reviews.

Property income and capital growth are, however, limited by two factors: first, rent review periods of 5 years; second, and more important, depreciation (see Section 3, below).

Table 2: Nottingham city centre retail property: rents, inflation and initial yields, 1910 - 1960

Years	Prime Rent Index (1)		Average Rent Index (2)		RPI (3)	Prime Initial Yields (4)	Gilts (5)
1910	100.00	43.30	100.00	38.20	94	5.00	3.10
1911	96.90		96.00		95	5.00	3.20
1912	95.40		92.90		98	5.00	3.30
1913	95.40		91.60		100	4.50	3.40
1914	95.40		91.60		101	6.50	3.30
1915	95.40		91.60		121	-	3.80
1916	95.40		91.60		143	-	4.30
1917	96.90		94.60		173	-	4.60
1918	99.20		99.30		199	6.75	4.40
1919	101.50		104.40		211	5.00	4.60
1920	104.60		109.80		244	5.00	5.30
1921	106.90		114.80		222	4.50	5.20
1922	109.20		120.50		179	5.50	4.40
1923	111.50		125.60		171	6.00	4.30
1924	118.50		132.30		172	6.25	4.40
1925	123.10		138.70		173	6.00	4.40
1926	127.70		148.80		169	5.50	4.60
1927	133.80		157.60		164	5.00	4.60
1928	140.00		168.40		163	4.00	4.50
1929	147.70		180.10		161	5.00	4.60
1930	153.80		198.70		155	6.00	4.50
1931	135.40		159.90		145	9.00	4.40
1932	135.40		158.90		141	8.00	3.70
1933	135.40		158.20		137	6.50	3.40
1934	135.40		160.30		138	6.50	3.10
1935	135.40		161.90		140	6.00	2.90
1936	135.40		166.70		144	6.00	2.90
1937	143.80		177.80		152	5.50	3.30
1938	152.30		187.20		153	5.00	3.40
1939	146.20		181.50		158	5.00	3.70
1940	140.00		172.10		179	7.50	3.40
1941	140.00		170.00		197	-	3.10
1942	140.00		170.00		210	-	3.00
1943	140.00		170.00		217	-	3.10
1944	140.00		170.40		222	7.00	3.10
1945	161.50		192.80		226	6.00	2.90
1946	230.80	100.00	262.00	100.00	236	5.00	2.60
1947		105.60		108.90	249	4.50	2.80
1948		110.20		116.00	268	4.50	3.20
1949		111.90		124.10	275	4.50	3.30
1950		114.10		131.40	283	4.50	3.50
1951		116.70		138.00	311	4.50	3.80
1952		123.30		146.30	338	5.00	4.20
1953		139.80		160.90	349	5.50	4.10
1954		158.60		170.00	355	5.20	3.80
1955		179.80		198.30	371	5.00	4.20
1956		200.00		224.50	389	5.50	4.70
1957		212.00		253.70	404	5.50	5.00
1958		222.60		276.50	416	5.50	5.00
1959		233.40		293.30	418	6.00	4.80
1960		242.70		308.30	422	6.00	6.40

Notes to Table 2:
(1), (2), (4) Compiled by Crosby from data obtained from a number of sources. Main source: Harlow Shelton & Co., Chartered Surveyors, Nottingham.

(3) National Income Expenditure and Output of the UK 1865 - 1965 (for reference, see Crosby, 1985).

(5) Abstract of British Historical Statistics and Second Abstract of British Historical Statistics (2½% Consols, undated stock, gross redemption yields) (for reference, see Crosby, 1985).

Psychic income

For many smaller investors property has an appeal unmatched by the alternatives. For some, this may be a prestige or even advertising value: for others, it may be the opportunity for exercising positive management and, while perhaps increasing return, offering self-employment. This may have a marginal downward impact upon the required initial yield.

Operating expenses

Once the purchase of an investment has been completed, the investor must face the prospect of continued expense necessitated by ownership. For bank deposits, such operating expenses are nil, apart from the investor's own time spent in checking accounts. For securities, the management of a given investment (rather than a portfolio) is again reduced to reading the financial press. For property, on the other hand, operating expenses derive from several sources. Repair and maintenance costs, insurance premiums, rent review fees, management (rent collection, periodic inspection, service management) fees, shortfalls in service charges, rates (in some circumstances), re-letting fees, refurbishment costs, dilapidations claims, and various legal expenses arising out of disputes with the public, tenants or adjoining owners contribute to a potentially high annual expenditure for the property investment owner, and may increase required yields.

Liquidity

Liquidity is the ease and certainty with which an asset can be converted to cash at, or close to, its market value. Bank deposits are almost perfectly liquid; gilts are usually convertible to cash within one day;

and equities may be transformed to cash within a week to a month. Property is relatively illiquid. A quick sale will not usually be possible unless a low price is accepted. Even then, the period between a decision to sell and receipt of cash can be as long as 3 months.

Contributing to property's illiquidity are three factors. Marketability describes the reserve of potential buyers for an investment and the speed and ease with which they may be contacted. For large property investments – buildings worth more than £10m, say – the number of potential buyers may be small. For unusual investments the potential market may be difficult to target and advertising may be highly inefficient. On the other hand, the stock exchange ensures the marketability of most gilts and equities.

The indivisibility of property as an investment contributes to its lack of marketability and therefore to its illiquidity. The possibility of sale of part of an investment reduces the impact of this problem and facilitates flexible financial management. Property can be physically divided, divided into freehold and leaseholds or split into time shares, but it remains in general a fundamentally indivisible investment, with a high minimum outlay. Until a unitised market becomes established the purchase and sale of small units of property investment will not normally be possible. This is not true of alternatives.

The transfer costs necessitated when a decision to sell is finally translated into cash are higher than those associated with the alternatives. Stamp duty, conveyancing fees and agents' fees on purchase and sale may total 3% and 2.5% of price respectively. A more likely transfer cost for equities is around 0.5% for a reasonable volume, and the analogous costs are likely to be less for gilts.

Illiquidity and its associates may therefore be said to be highest for property in comparison with the chosen alternative. It has been argued (Fraser, 1985) that the infrequency of property trading as compared with trading frequency in the stock market reduces the importance of this factor, but infrequency of trading probably *results* from illiquidity. The fact remains that cash tied up in property is, pound for pound, less liquid than cash tied up elsewhere. This has two implications: firstly, it increases the chances of a company becoming financially embarrassed and put out of business by lenders; secondly, it decreases the chances of attractive alternatives being acquired. For property companies, the illiquidity of property may be said to be more of a problem than it is for the larger institutions, but in general illiquidity should increase required initial yields for property.

Tax efficiency

The tax efficiency of an investment refers to the degree to which a gross return is reduced to a net return for the individual investor. Given the different and complex tax positions of individuals, institutions and companies alike, it is impossible to make generalisations about the relative tax efficiency of a real estate investment. However, tax warrants thorough attention in each individual appraisal, and is consistently under-rated as a factor in property investment analysis.

Risk

Most investments are traded in an atmosphere of uncertainty, so that it is not possible to predict with accuracy what the level of return will be. Even fixed interest gilts held to redemption produce a return which is uncertain in real terms and dependent upon future inflation levels for purchasing power.

Some finance texts view risk as the major determinant of return. Modern portfolio theory contributes to this importance by regarding the investment decision as a trade-off between expected returns and risk (see Branch, 1985).

Reilly (1985) defines risk simply as "uncertainty regarding the expected rate of return from an investment". While there is nothing intrinsically unattractive about uncertainty when the expected rate of return may be much higher or much lower than expected, conventional wisdom is (as suggested above) that investors are on average risk-averse. For example, Brigham (1985) states:

> Most investors are indeed risk-averse. Since this is a well-documented fact, we shall assume risk aversion throughout the remainder of the book.

Downside risk is typically of more practical concern than its upside equivalent. Risk aversion therefore implies that a normal but narrow distribution of possible returns from an investment is preferable to another with greater spread, because upside and downside risk cannot be said to cancel. While upside risk may imply super-performance of an investment or a portfolio in any one year, and this is usually (but not always) welcome, downside risk may imply liquidation of a company or fund through insolvency, the effects of which cannot be matched by equal chances of high returns.

There are many sources of property risk, some unique to this investment form (see Baum and Crosby, 1988). They include, in particular, the chance that the tenant will affect return adversely by his actions and the chance of changes in the law, in taxation rules or in

planning policy which directly or indirectly affect investment returns.
More relevant to the subject matter of this book, however, are sector
risk and structural risk.

Sector risk

Sector risk is the chance that differential sectoral price movements
affect the subject investment. Such a risk is present in the ordinary
share market, where the choice of sector may be vital. Electricals may
underperform industrials and chemicals; within that sector, micro-
electronics may underperform household goods.

A property's sector risk is more sharply focused than this. Given
the *lumpiness* of property investment, property is particularly prone
to sector risks in two dimensions. First, there is a risk of a performance
differential between office, shop and industrial sectors. For example,
in the period 1977 to 1985 industrials, on the whole, performed poorly
in relation to shops (see Table 1).

Second, the locational factor provides a dimension of risk which is
not exactly parallelled elsewhere. To illustrate this, Table 3 shows
regional variations in rental value and capitalisation rates between 1977
and 1985.

Table 3: Shop rents and yields, 1977-1985

	1977	1978	1979	1980	1981	1982	1983	1984	1985
Rent index									
All shops	100	117	147	170	181	195	203	219	244
North	100	119	166	187	202	224	230	255	282
South East	100	109	138	171	196	206	222	236	265
Midlands	100	115	137	161	176	202	210	221	250
Scotland	100	121	152	188	192	191	194	200	221
London	100	121	147	159	157	160	165	184	203
Average yields (%)									
All shops	6.1	5.3	4.8	4.8	4.7	4.7	5.0	4.8	4.8
North	5.9	5.1	4.5	4.5	4.4	4.4	4.6	4.5	4.5
South East	5.6	4.8	4.3	4.3	4.1	4.1	4.4	4.1	4.1
Midlands	6.1	5.3	4.7	4.7	4.6	4.6	4.8	4.6	4.6
Scotland	5.9	5.4	5.3	4.9	4.8	4.8	5.3	4.8	4.7
London	6.8	5.9	5.4	5.4	5.4	5.4	5.7	5.7	5.7

Source: Investors Chronicle Hillier Parker Rent Index and Average
        Yields

To illustrate this more simply, the annual rate of return on shop property in the North and London performing in line with the regional rent movements and yield fluctuations would be as shown in Table 4.

Table 4: Notional property performance, North and London, (%) 1978 - 1985

	1978	1979	1980	1981	1982	1983	1984	1985	Average
North	37.6	58.1	12.6	10.5	10.9	-1.8	13.3	10.6	17.75
London	39.4	32.7	8.2	-1.3	1.9	-2.3	11.5	10.3	11.68

Source: Table 3
Note: Assumes annual reviews

Although shop average yields have fallen since 1977, industrial and office yields have risen. The average industrial yield shows a greater variation than shops by region. The south east industrial average yield was 8.8% in 1977 and by 1985 had returned to the same figure. The industrial yield in the north was also 8.8% in 1977 but had risen to 11.9% by 1985 (May) and rents had remained static since 1980 with corresponding real declines in value. An industrial property in the north bought in 1977 and having performed like the index would show an eight year average annual average return of just 1.4% between May 1977 and 1985. A property in the south east would have an annual average return of 10.4% over the same period. Sectoral risk clearly applies to both property region and property type.

Structural risk

Structural risk is the chance of high repair costs, maintenance costs, refurbishment and, eventually, rebuilding becoming necessary. Such risks are not parallelled in other markets other than indirectly, and even then in a highly diversified manner. (For example, there may be structural risk attached to the performance of ordinary shares in a heavy industry company with one old manufacturing plant, but this type of risk would be much reduced in the case of a chain of retail shops where a spread of units (if owned freehold) would diversify such risk and reduce its impact on performance.)

It is not currently easy to generalise about the life of building types. However, freehold interests in prime shop units are much less prone to structural risk than are modern industrial units. Shops are often simple cubes, the responsibility for much of the renewal of which is passed to tenants, while for industrial buildings the type of construction, the nature of occupation and the impact of technology upon industry reduce economic life. It is also clear that land is less likely to *depreciate* in normal circumstances, so that property investments with a proportionately larger land value are less prone to structural risk. Office buildings in the City of London are thus less prone to structural risk than are similar buildings in Houston, Texas where land values are less protected by physical boundaries and planning restrictions, and are in any event lower due to the relative eminence of the City of London as a financial centre.

Other structural risks may be passed on to tenants through full repairing and insuring leases, but the ultimate responsibility for obsolescence and fundamental defects rests with the property owner who consequently shoulders a risk unique to this form of investment.

Money or real risk?

Risk is typically measured by volatility, and may be analysed in terms of the volatility of money income (the possibility of variations in the actual income and capital returns from the expected) or in terms of the volatility of real income (the possibility of variations in the real value of actual and capital returns from the expected). The choice is a significant one and depends greatly upon the liabilities of the investor. A predictive comparison of property with (for example) fixed interest gilts is simpler on the former basis, while a comparison with index-linked gilts is simpler when predicated on the latter basis.

Real risk is arguably a preferable basis for investment comparison. However, property investment analysis is likely to be more capable of comparable interpretation against other capital market investments in a monetary, rather than real, framework, and this is the assumption underlying this work.

Individual asset or portfolio risk?

Markowitz developed a portfolio model (Markowitz, 1959) which showed how risk may be reduced within a portfolio by combining assets whose returns demonstrate less than perfect positive correlation. Given that the typical investor is risk-averse, the combination of two or more investments whose returns fluctuate over time and in different conditions but in opposite directions can reduce risk without at the same time reducing return. Thus, if it can be shown that as industrial properties decline in value shops increase in value and *vice versa*, a two-asset property portfolio is superior to a portfolio comprised exclusively of either individual asset. The investor de-values a risky asset; two negatively correlated risky assets in combination would therefore be worth more than the sum of the two individual values.

Sharpe (1964) showed that it is unnecessary to compute correlations between all asset types where investors hold large diversified portfolios, in other words market portfolios. Volatility in relation to the market becomes the only risk type which will be compensated by high return. Beta (β) is the measure of systematic risk, the volatility of an investment in relation to the market portfolio (that is, a portfolio comprising every known asset weighted in terms of market value). A beta of 1.0 implies that, as the market increases in value by 10% , the expected value of the investment increases by 10%. A beta of 2.0 implies that as the market increases in value by 10% the expected value of the investment increases by 20%; a beta of 0.5 implies that as the market increases in value by 10% the expected value of the investment increases by 5%; and so on.

The return on a risky investment should comprise the risk free rate plus a risk premium (Rp) which reflects the systematic risk of the investment relative to the market. Where an investment is twice as risky as the market, the expectation is that it should earn twice the risk premium. The measure of this relative riskiness is beta (β). Thus (where Rm is the return on the market) the return on a risky investment (Ra) is given by the following:

$$Ra = RFR + \beta (Rm - RFR)$$
$$Rm - RFR = Rp$$

Therefore, $Ra = RFR + \beta (Rp)$

Empirical studies in the UK have shown that Rp has in recent years been close to 9% (Brown, 1985). The risk free rate is estimated in nominal terms and is based on the return on short-term Treasury Bills, or the redemption yield on short-dated government bonds. Assuming a nominal risk-free rate of 10%, the expected return on the market can be estimated as follows:

$$Rm = RFR + Rp$$
$$= 0.10 + 0.09$$
$$= \underline{19\%}$$

The required return on risky investments can then be calculated given a value for beta of the individual asset against the market. Brown (1985) made an attempt to estimate betas for the three major sectors of the property market. However, there are three major difficulties in such an approach.

1. Data which enable the estimation of beta against a market are artificially smoothed by the use of valuation, rather than trading price, data.
2. The estimation of beta against the market requires a market index which includes property, but no such index exists.

3. Property investors cannot hold the market, so that it cannot be assumed that the market is dominated by fully diversified investors for whom the relevant risk measure is beta.

Baum (1989b) presents a fuller discussion of the problems inherent in a CAPM approach. In summary, it appears that the absolute downside variability of the property asset continues to be relevant, and that CAPM is not applicable in a property context. For example, Hargitay (1983) and Ward (1979) confirm the caution which must be exercised in applying the capital asset pricing model to the property market given current data and index constraints. This book therefore applies traditional risk measures.

3. The importance of depreciation and obsolescence

Property is an investment class which competes for the allocation of institutional funds with cash and securities, including equities and both conventional and index-linked gilts. Its appeal lies in its ability to enhance portfolio returns and/or to reduce portfolio risk.

Return

The ability of property to enhance portfolio returns is dependant upon its reaction to inflation, its potential for producing a real return, its occasional monopoly rewards and its suitability for leverage. This ability is, however, constrained by rent review patterns and, more importantly, by a factor which, for the moment, shall be called depreciation and obsolescence. In the early 1980's the perceived attractiveness of property as a growth asset was somewhat checked, and it is argued in Chapter 3 that the major factor in this re-assessment was a growing fear of depreciation and/or obsolescence, with little attempt made to distinguish the two. Chapters 1 and 2 of this book follow a similar practice, whereby the terms are used interchangeably. In Chapter 4 a distinction is derived, and the remainder of the work maintains that definitional distinction.

To state the matter simply, buildings wear out, and in the 1980's they were probably wearing out more quickly than at any time previously. Realisation of this caused yields in the more sensitive areas of the market (provincial offices and all industrials) to respond by moving upwards, and the result was extremely poor, and even negative, property performance in the context of a strong equity market performance in the early and mid 1980's. Table 4 contrasts the performance of shops and industrials in the period 1980 to 1984, and raises the possibility that a special factor affected the latter. This prompts an interest in property depreciation and obsolescence and raises one of the two major questions addressed in this book. That first question is: is it possible to find out more about the causes of depreciation and obsolescence, so that its impact may be limited by developers and property managers?

Risk

Property may reduce portfolio risk because it is poorly correlated with other assets and because it exhibits low volatility, especially in real terms (see Baum, 1989b). However, this argument for holding real estate in a portfolio is questioned when property risk is further examined. Firstly, sector risk has been higher in recent years. Arguably due to depreciation and obsolescence, the performance of offices and industrials together moved significantly away from the performance of shops in the early and middle 1980's. Secondly, as a result of rapid technological change and severe changes in the structure of the UK economy, the structural risk of property investment has increased considerably in recent years. This increase in the potential and actual volatility of property, arguably depreciation-led, creates inefficiencies and uncertainties, so that the return on an investment may prove to be higher or lower than expected, creating (by definition) a risk which has to be taken into account. It is stated in Chapter 2 that this is typically achieved by means of a risk-adjusted discount rate, but this raises the second major question which is addressed by this research. The question is: can property investment decisions be improved by a framework which, while acknowledging that depreciation is a risky variable, attempts an explicit estimation of its impact upon cash flow?

The CALUS report and beyond

Two major questions are posed immediately above. They concern the causes of depreciation and the possibility of making an explicit allowance for depreciation in property investment decision models. Each question needs to be posed, because there has been little examination of the impact of depreciation and obsolescence on property investments to date.

The major exception to this is the CALUS report (Salway, 1986), the first major UK work to be devoted to building depreciation and its various effects. While not specific to property investment, this work made considerable reference to it, and is therefore more fully referred to later in this book, especially in Chapter 3.

The CALUS report identified the two areas within which further advances were most urgently needed. These were:

  i to expose the forces behind depreciation; and
  ii to set up analytical models which enable decision makers to make due allowance for it.

These questions broadly equate with the two questions posed earlier in this section. They are the two basic questions which drive the research described in this book.

These two aims require two pieces of work. Firstly, probably most important and certainly involving the expenditure of the greater time and resource, this research sets up a model for classifying the forces behind depreciation (Chapter 4) and describes two empirical studies of offices and industrials which measure the influence of these forces on property investment worth (Chapters 5, 6 and 7). Secondly, it is necessary to establish a framework for the analysis of property investments which can accommodate an informed anticipation of depreciation. This is dealt with by establishing a basic model in Chapter 2 and later by building on this work by developing a depreciation-sensitive model.

Chapters 1 to 4 are grouped by their contextual nature and form Part 1 of this book (Context). The central empirical work is described in Chapters 5 to 7, which form Part 2 (Analysis). The analytical model is constructed in Chapter 8 and conclusions are drawn in Chapter 9. These form Part 3 (Models and Conclusions).

Chapter 2

Cash flow models for property investment analysis

1. Comparative investment analysis

An examination of the alternative investment types against which property may be appraised is driven by the investment policies of the UK's major investors, the larger insurance companies and pension funds, which have in the last two decades pursued a policy of portfolio diversification by retaining a mix of cash, ordinary shares and fixed interest gilts but increasing holdings of property and more recently, of index-linked gilts.

This has resulted indirectly in the property valuation profession having been made the subject of scrutiny by professionals in other capital markets (for example, see Greenwell and Co., 1976). This critical examination led to the appearance in 1980 of a report (Trott, 1980) which re-examined property investment appraisal techniques and found them deficient.

As a result of these and other coincident publications, property advisers have been placed under increasing pressure to provide analytical, defensible and accurate appraisals that are capable of comparative interpretation. This has to be contrasted with the valuer's traditional initial yield model, which leads to great difficulties in cross-investment comparative analysis.

The initial yield is an apparently simple yet effectively complex measure of the quality of an investment. Used for analysis the model is:

$$\text{initial yield} = \frac{\text{current income}}{\text{price}}$$

where current income and price are given and where initial yield incorporates a series of implicit measurements, of (for example) a risk free opportunity cost, expected income and capital growth, liquidity, operating expenses, psychic income, risk and other factors (see Chapter 1). This does not advance a comparative analysis, now regarded as a necessary quality of a property analysis model, for the following reasons.

1. The return on other investments may be a measure against which a property investment should be appraised. For example the redemption yield on conventional gilts is generally accepted as an indication of the equated yield/target rate which should be used in property appraisals based on discounted cash flow (DCF).
2. The return on other investments may be a guide to the future value of property. If conventional gilts yield 16% when prime shops yield 3.5%, when little or no rental growth is currently expected (as in 1982), it is possible to conclude that prime shops will fall in price, as indeed they did in 1983 (see Table 3). Advice to a vendor or purchaser should reflect that view.
3. Subject to 1 above, the return on other investments may be a guide to the implied necessary future performance of property. For example, levels of implied rental and .capital growth can be computed given information regarding redemption yields on bonds and initial yields on property. Such information will aid the investor's choice between alternative property investments.

2. The development of explicit cash flow models

Formats

Explicit cash flow models for the analysis of property investment risk and return have been developed and explored quite fully in recent years in order to progress property analysis towards a capital market comparative framework.

Marshall (1976) developed an early analytical model (which he termed equated yield analysis) relying upon the explicit projection of cash flows from an investment and discounting them at a risk-adjusted opportunity cost rate (equated yield). Some debate over the implicit treatment of the expected resale price was created by the use of the equated yield to discount income flows after the end of the analysis period (usually 30 years in Marshall's examples) implying a cessation of growth after that period and, arguably, an implicit allowance for depreciation.

This explicit format has continued to be used as one of three cash flow based models which attempt rational and comparative interpretation. Korpacz and Roth (1983) illustrate by a fully developed case study their explicit cash flow model; Robinson (1985 and 1986) illustrates the use of spreadsheets as ideal technology for the model; and the practical UK application of explicit cash flow analysis is demonstrated for example by Baum and Butler (1986), Mason (1986) and Miles (1986).

Alongside the development of explicit models, two conventional-format alternatives have also been published. These are the *rational model* of Sykes (1981) and Sykes and McIntosh (1982) and the *real value model* of Crosby (1985). The three approaches are consistent in results obtained (that is, they equate in the simple case); all represent a useful advance on conventional practice. (See Baum (1984), Baum (1985) and Baum and Crosby (1988) for a full comparison of these approaches.) All may be described as cash flow models.

Variables in a cash flow model

Property investment analysis is designed to estimate the worth of a property investment to an investor. Worth may be expressed in three forms. Where the price of an investment is known, for example in a retrospective analysis after a sale, or where negotiations for a purchase by private treaty have neared completion, the worth of the investment must be expressed either as an expected rate of return or an excess value over the price (net present value) at a given target rate. Where the price is unknown, for example where an investment is to be sold by auction, the analysis is aimed at an assessment of the capital value of the investment, or the maximum price that can be paid, given a target rate of return.

The return from a property investment is a function of income, capital return and psychic income. No attempt is made to measure the latter, and shorter leaseholds may not produce a capital return. Thus gross cash flow will be made up of income and (perhaps) capital. The income may increase at reviews. Estimation of a capital return depends upon the timing of a sale so that it is necessary to estimate a likely holding period. Holding costs will be incurred during the period of ownership, and these will need to be estimated. Purchase and sale transfer costs will be payable; at each rent review a fee will be payable; letting or reletting costs may have to be faced; and management fees may be incurred.

Taxes on income and capital gain will be charged. Leaseholders may be faced with dilapidations claims. The income may be inclusive, so that the investor pays rates out of the rent received; and a service charge may not cover the cost of service provision. Properties have to be repaired and refurbished.

The estimation of values for each of these factors will produce an explicit net cash flow projection. If the price is known, the rate of return becomes the dependent variable in the analysis. If the price is not known, the target rate has to be added to the above list of independent variables, the capital value becoming the independent variable. The same model should be able to accommodate either variation. All variables are briefly considered below.

The holding period

For purely technical reasons – that is, to avoid an infinitely long cash flow projection in a freehold analysis – a finite holding period is utilised in the analysis model. For freeholds this implies the assumption of a resale or a reversion to constant growth, using Gordon's growth model (Brigham, 1985), while for leaseholds the holding period will usually equate with the remaining term.

The overriding concern in the choice of holding period must be the intentions of the investor. Discussions with the investor might reveal his likely or intended ownership period; where no intention to sell is apparent, the holding period becomes arbitrary. In either case, there are reasons for coinciding the resale date with the end of an occupation lease or a rent review period. This reflects likely practice, as there is a suspicion that fuller prices are achieved immediately after review because the purchaser's risk is reduced. While periods of 10 or 15 years are often settled on for convenience, it should be noted that slight changes in holding period return may be achieved by shortening or lengthening the holding period, and this type of exercise is one of several uses of a model.

Resale price

In the case of freeholds and long leaseholds the selection of a holding period will trigger the assumption of a resale at that date. The resale price to be projected is the most likely selling price at that date. If the most common method of market pricing is the years' purchase method, and given that the sale will usually coincide with a review, the freehold resale price is given by:

Estimated rental value (ERV) x YP in perpetuity,

or: $$\frac{\text{ERV}}{\text{Capitalisation rate (k), at resale date}}$$

This requires the projection of two variables: ERV at resale and k at resale.

Estimated rental value (ERV)

A projection of rental value at the point of resale in property investment analysis need not, of course, be based upon a market-implied growth rate. While this may be a guide, it should be remembered that the implied growth rate is an average rate in perpetuity; it is also net of depreciation. This raises several issues which are discussed in Chapter 8.

Capitalisation rate (k)

The estimation of a capitalisation rate for the subject property 10 or 15 years hence requires forecasts. Firstly, yields for the type of property under consideration may be expected to change over the period. If so, the extent to which the market yield will change must be estimated. Secondly, the movement in yield of the subject property against an index of yields of such properties in a frozen state over the holding period, in other words the extent of depreciation likely to be suffered by an ageing building, needs to be estimated. Again, this is developed in Chapter 8.

Gross income flow

Forecasting gross income flow or rental growth over the holding period is important both in the estimation of the rental flow and in the prediction of the resale price. Forecasting a variable such as this might be based upon any of three methods: extrapolation of time series data, identifying relationships, or a combined approach.

Extrapolation of time series data

From a time series of rental value, it may be possible to identify a long term trend but a cyclical pattern will almost certainly obscure this to some extent. In addition there may be non-recurring influences – rent freezes, for example – which need to be smoothed away. Extrapolation of the time series therefore takes into account both cyclical variations and the long-term trend. (See, for example, Field and MacGregor (1987).)

Identifying causal relationships

Forecasting the future by the analysis of past relationships is an integral forecasting tool. The analyst forms a hypothesis by using statistical tests of data. For example, the lagged impact of consumer spending (the independent variable) upon retail property rental value (the dependent variable) might be tested by comparing the two factors over time and measuring the correlation between the two. If correlation is high, a simple prediction may be made. The ideal situation for the forecaster would be where the independent variable is seen to move in advance of the dependant variable. Analysis of the business cycle is often undertaken to find indicators which lead the economy and those leading indicators form the basis of models which predict changes in the important economic variables.

A combined approach

The most common method of forecasting utilised in the property market is an approach which combines extrapolation with a causal analysis, almost certainly in an informal framework, although formal econometric models are gaining popularity. The analyst is likely to base projections primarily on extrapolation coloured by causal influences (the forthcoming supply of new property in the sector, for example). (Forecasting cash flows is discussed further in Section 4 of this chapter.)

Regular expenses

Implicit within the gross cash flow from a property investment is a series of regularly recurring expenses. These include management costs, either fees charged by an agent or the time of staff. In the former case they may be based upon a percentage of gross rents; in the latter, they need more careful estimation, and may have to be increased over time. Repairs and maintenance will normally be covered, like insurance, by the tenant's obligations under a full repairing and insuring lease; if not, they must be accounted for, as must the exceptional burden of rates.

While the investor who provides services, for example to the common parts of a multi-tenanted office building or shopping centre, will usually expect to recover these expenses in a service charge, the amount received may not quite match the cost of provision through a lagging effect or other causes, in which case an allowance needs to be made.

All expenses not tied to rent must be subject to an allowance for anticipated cost inflation.

Periodic expenses

While most leases place the burden of normal repairs upon tenants, landlords will expect to have to bear some expenditure from time to time, and the burden of repair is effectively shared. In addition to this, improvements may be necessary to make the property marketable.

Thus at the end of an occupation lease the investor will be faced with the prospect of redeveloping, refurbishing, repairing or redecorating the property and the leaseholder may be faced with a claim for dilapidations. If the lease end falls within the holding period, the prospect must be allowed for, again with an inflation factor. This is dealt with in Chapter 8.

Fees

In order to strip out all costs to leave a net return estimate, acquisition fees and sale fees at the end of the holding period need to be removed from the cash flow. These will normally be based upon the purchase and sale prices.

Rent review fees, based upon the new rent agreed, need to be allowed for at each review, and re-leasing fees, again based on the new rent agreed, have to be provided for at the lease end. Advertising costs may be additional to both sale and re-leasing fees. VAT should be added to all expenses where appropriate.

Taxes

Property investment analysis for the individual investor or fund can, and should, be absolutely specific regarding the tax implications of the purchase. Thus capital and writing down allowances should be taken into account where appropriate. Income or corporation tax should be removed from the income flow. Capital gains tax payable upon resale can be estimated given an estimation of purchase price, sale price, intervening expenditure, holding period and intervening inflation, all of which are central to a model of this nature.

The target rate of return

The principal purpose of property investment analysis is the facilitation of decision-making. The basic criterion for decision-making in investment, risk considerations apart, is the expected or required rate of return (IRR). This is normally termed the target rate of return.

The target rate should be based upon the return required by the investor to compensate for the loss of capital employed in the project which could have been employed elsewhere, that is the opportunity cost of capital (for example, the redemption yield on similar maturity gilts). It may be adjusted for risk (in which case it becomes a risk-adjusted discount rate).

It is common to see no distinction between the required return on borrowed and equity funds. This is, however, unrealistic. Financial markets cannot be assumed to be efficient, so that the opportunity cost of equity to an equity investor such as a pension fund and the actual cost of equity (dividends required by investors) to an equity/debt investor such as a property company may not equate with the actual cost of borrowing capital. Consequently, the analyst should rely upon the concept of opportunity cost (and not the actual cost of capital) in the estimation of target rate.

In certain circumstances the cost of borrowing may be taken into account by using the weighted average cost of capital. For a fuller discussion of the weighted average cost of capital see Brigham (1985) and Brealey and Myers (1985). The target rate is discussed in more depth in Section 4 of this chapter, but is treated simplistically in the analyses exemplified in this book.

3. Risk/return analysis

A present value or internal rate of return analysis based upon income and expense projection is a first base level of property investment analysis. Analysts are increasingly forced to use market analysis to predict the uncertain, that is to make an estimate of the cash flow likely to be produced by the investment. This element of uncertainty demands another level of decision-aiding analysis. However, risk analysis, well explored in financial theory, has not yet been the subject of comprehensive examination in the real estate sector, and neither acceptable definitions nor empirical tests of real estate risk have yet been developed. There is an absence of reported data regarding the riskiness of individual real estate investments, both in terms of quantum and source (although developments are being made: see for example the research of Brown (1985)).

NPV or IRR?

All levels of decision technology for real estate investment discussed herein are based on DCF analysis and utilise a return measure. Estimation of return may be by net present value (NPV) or internal rate of return (IRR). These alternatives are assessed in detail in Baum and Crosby (1988). The conclusion reached is that NPV is clearly preferable as a decision aid, even though IRR has attractions for practitioners. Both NPV and IRR are utilised in the cash flow model illustrated below, but the preferred output is NPV.

Example

This simple example forms the basis of further work in Chapter 8. It shows the use of the following variables: holding period, resale price, gross income flow, fees (rent review in this case) and target rate. The example ignores regular expenses, periodic expenses and taxes, which are nonetheless easily incorporated in this format.

Assume a property is for sale at a price of £800 per square foot. The current estimated rental value is £40 per annum per square foot.

The average redemption yield on long dated gilts is currently around 9%. A 2% risk premium is required over this rate.

A fee of 7% of the new rent will be paid at each (5-yearly) rent review. Rental growth until the first rent review is estimated at 8% per annum and this rate of growth is projected to remain constant over reviews 2 and 3.

The current capitalisation rate (implied by a rental value of £40 against a price of £800) is 5%. This is forecast to remain constant over the holding period.

Projected rental values are therefore as follows: at the first review, the current ERV will have risen from £40 to £59; at the second review, this will become £86; at the third review (that is, the end of the holding period) the rental value will be £127. This will not influence the rental income but will determine the resale value of the property at the end of the holding period. This is given by:

$$\frac{\text{ERV at review 3 (year 15)}}{\text{year 15 capitalisation rate}}$$

Given a risk premium of 2% over the gilt yield of 9% a target rate of 11% is used to calculate NPV.

The cash flow shown details the combined effect of these projections and the deduction of rent review fees at years 5, 10 and 15. The analysis shows that the decision is to buy, because the IRR exceeds the target rate and the NPV is positive. This simple example is used as the basis of the illustration of risk analysis in the remainder of this chapter and also forms the basis of the depreciation-sensitive model developed in Chapter 8.

DATA	
Price	£800.00
ERV	£40.00
Gilt redemption yield	9.00%
Risk premium	2.00%
Rent review fee	7.00%
Rental growth review 1	8.00%
Rental growth review 2	8.00%
Rental growth review 3	8.00%
Year 0 capitalisation rate	5.00%
Year 15 capitalisation rate	5.00%

PROJECTIONS	
	(£)
ERV, review 1	59
ERV, review 2	86
ERV, review 3	127
Net resale value	2,538

ANALYSIS	
Target rate (%)	11.00
NPV (£)	113.00
IRR (%)	12.27

CASH FLOW STATEMENT				
Year	Capital £	Income £	Outflow £	Net cash £
0	(800)			(800)
1		40		40
2		40		40
3		40		40
4		40		40
5		40	(4)	36
6		59		59
7		59		59
8		59		59
9		59		59
10		59	(6)	53
11		86		86
12		86		86
13		86		86
14		86		86
15	2,538	86	(9)	2,615

Sensitivity analysis: a first exploration of risk and return

Risk is defined by Reilly (1985) as "uncertainty regarding the expected rate of return from an investment". In the example the investment suffers from two major uncertainties. These are the estimated growth in rental value and the anticipated resale capitalisation rate.

Sensitivity analysis was developed as a means of identifying the independent variable changes in which cause the greatest change in the dependent variable. Many other simple explorations of risk are made possible by this technique.

In the example, it is a straightforward matter to alter either of these variables by the same relative amount and to test the effect on the result. For example, a one-tenth improvement in rental growth is slightly more beneficial than a one-tenth fall in resale capitalisation rate. Alternatively, it may be useful to alter the variables by an equally likely amount. A one-tenth improvement in rental growth may be as likely as a one-<u>twentieth</u> fall in resale capitalisation rate, in which case the relative effect of these variations would be, of course, to confirm the extra sensitivity of the result to rental growth.

Sensitivity analysis therefore allows a more informed decision to be made. It does, however, fail to address a vital point. What is the probability of the possible variations becoming fact? This will surely qualify the above analysis, as it requires an element of qualitative or subjective judgement. The best outcome in the case of alternative investment A may be less profitable than the best outcome in alternative B: but the latter may be much less likely than the former. This element of risk must be taken into account in a full analysis. It is not enough to say what could happen; it is necessary to qualify such hypotheses.

Risk adjustment techniques

Both the potential variation and the chances of variation in the outcome from that which is expected should be taken into account in a full risk-return analysis utilising methods of varying formality. Such methods are widely practised, both consciously and unconsciously, in both the capital markets and in real estate.

Three manifestations of risk-adjustment techniques relevant in this context are the risk adjusted discount rate; the certainty equivalent technique; and a hybrid of these, suitable for UK property investment analysis, termed the sliced income method. These are described in detail in Baum and Crosby (1988). For the remainder of this book, particularly in Chapter 8, the risk-adjusted discount rate is utilised.

Risk-adjusted discount rate

Whether by NPV or IRR, a point return estimate has to incorporate allowances for risks (defined here as variance of possible returns) when used to choose between alternatives. Choosing on the basis of IRRs alone where risks differ presumes indifference to risk. Given that investors are risk averse a choice on the basis of IRR must therefore involve a risk adjustment.

Either the discount rate or the income may be adjusted to take account of risk. The use of the risk-adjusted discount rate is to adjust the former and is derived from Fisher (1930). The interest (or discount) rate (I) can be constructed from the following function:

$$(1 + i)\,(1 + d)\,(1 + r) - 1$$

where i represents a return for time preference, d represents a return for expected inflation and r represents a return for risk. The risk free rate (RFR), 9% in the example, is a function of i and d:

$$RFR = (1 + i)\,(1 + d) - 1,$$
$$\text{so}\quad RADR = (1 + r)\,(1 + RFR) - 1.$$

This is the risk-adjusted discount rate. The greater the amount of perceived risk, the higher is RFR. This risk adjustment method is used in the example shown above.

Note that this is not the way the risk-adjusted discount rate (RADR) is normally constructed in practice. Instead, the RADR is usually found by RFR + r. The difference is usually small, and can be shown to be unimportant as the choice of r is arbitrary. In the example RFR = 9% and r = 2%. $(1 + RFR)\,(1 + r) - 1 = 11.18\%$; RFR + r = 11%. Such fine distinction in the RADR would normally be pointless.

The use of risk-adjusted discount rates implies that more return is required to compensate for greater risk. How much more is impossible to determine objectively; this depends upon the risk-return indifference curve of the investor, a subjective matter.

4. Conclusions

Implicit and explicit models

The continuing shift away from implicit property valuation and analysis models toward explicit cash flow projections might not produce better valuations and analyses. One benefit that has unarguably flowed, however, is the exposure of relevant variables for analysis.

The relationship between implicit and explicit models can be represented by a simple equation (loosely Gordon's growth model). Where k represents the all-risks yield (initial yield for a fully let property), e represents an overall return (redemption yield if a sale is envisaged) and g represents income growth, then (*ceteris paribus*) the left hand side of Equation (1) represents an all risks yield approach while the right hand side of the equation represents a growth explicit model.

$$k = e - g \qquad (1)$$

Fisher (1930) allows an expansion of this model. The overall return on an investment (e) is a reward for three factors. These are p, liquidity preference, d, anticipated inflation, and r, a risk premium.

Hence, $k = p + d + r - g$ (2)

This model holds for all assets. It is an extremely useful representation of the variables that property analysts are now beginning to struggle with. However, given that property analysis is more commonly based on nominal returns, d is not typically exposed and the model becomes as shown in Equation 3.

$$k = (p + d) + r - g \qquad (3)$$

(p + d) is a risk-free inflation-prone opportunity cost rate (RFR) traditionally derived from the redemption yield on conventional gilts. (This is faulty, as the risk of inflation being other than as expected is ignored, but this represents the popular approach.)

Hence, $k = RFR + r - g$ (4)

The importance of Equation 4, faulty though it is, is that it exposes r and g as the two variables currently requiring exploration in the property context. While k and RFR are derived from market evidence, r, a property risk premium over gilts, requires theoretical and empirical work at the market, sector and individual property level, and g, estimated rental growth, is the most difficult variable to deal with, requiring considerably more research and expertise.

Unresolved issues

Much recent debate has correctly centred on major variables in an explicit model the very purpose of which is the exposure of those variables for analysis.

1. *The discount or target rate* was the subject of Brown's doctoral work (Brown 1985), which included an adaptation of modern portfolio theory for the assessment of target rates for sectors of the commercial property market. Fraser (1986) argued for a radical approach to the estimation of the target rate, implying a negative risk premium.

   Many other academics and practitioners have adopted a 2% premium over the redemption yield on long dated gilts as the target rate for all property investments. This is patently simplistic. Lack of agreement between more advanced commentators leaves this as an important issue to be addressed in an explicit framework.

2. *The forecast income pattern* is usually modelled by a constant rate of rental growth, which also becomes impounded into the projected resale price. Market valuation models avoid this problem by tying income forecasts to an implied *market* expectation, utilising a formula which relates the three variables of target rate, initial yield and rental growth. Crosby (1985) clearly shows that the subjectivity involved in the choice of target rate does not greatly impact upon a *valuation* as its effect is cancelled by the rate of rental growth implied. As target rate (e) increases, the rate of growth (g) will fall, given a value for the market determined initial yield (k) and the broad relationship shown in Equation 1 above.

This is, however, of no use in a property investment *analysis* which is primarily for the purpose of aiding a decision to purchase or sell an investment, in other words to assess a subjective value which differs from the market estimate. Both target rate and expected growth (or otherwise) in income are variables which must be subjectively assessed.

A third independent variable?

This is the pre-depreciation state of the art. However, there is a growing perception that depreciation and obsolescence have to be accounted for in property appraisal models:

There has been much discussion in the property investment market. . . of the problems associated with obsolescence and its effect on property values. . . There has been comparatively little thought given to the means of analysing its effect. There is a clear need for the profession to address this aspect of the problem. . . (Debenham, Tewson and Chinnocks, 1985)

Depreciation and obsolescence therefore require exploration. The problem was referred to in Chapter 1 in two contexts.

Firstly, it appears to impact upon income (and capital) growth (g). In building a cash flow model for property investment analysis, this effect must be taken into account. The basic model presented in Section 2 of this chapter is a simple framework upon which may be constructed the modifications demanded by depreciation.

The second context within which depreciation becomes relevant is property investment risk (r). Given that knowledge is imperfect, should depreciation be treated as a variable capable of deterministic evaluation, as a risk, or as both? Section 3 of this chapter presents alternative risk/return analysis techniques for the individual investment which will provide the basis for analysis using a depreciation-sensitive model. Chapter 8 develops such a model.

This is not, however, the major objective. Chapters 3 to 7 attempt to provide a fuller understanding of the nature of depreciation which will inform decision-making. Chapter 8 then facilitates a fuller exploration of the impact of depreciation, whether it be treated as a deterministic variable, as a risk, or as both.

Chapter 3

Depreciation: a new variable

1. The CALUS report

In 1986 the College of Estate Management published a Research Report (The CALUS Report) titled *Depreciation of Commercial Property* (Salway, 1986). This report described research carried out in 1984/5 which was largely a response to concerns raised in 1982 (Bowie, 1982; see Section 2 below). Those concerns are listed as follows.

1. There was an awareness amongst those involved in the property industry that the useful life of many commercial buildings was becoming shorter. It was realised that if this was the case there might be significant implications for property valuation and management practices.
2. There appeared to be some uncertainty in the property market as to whether the prices paid for investment properties fully reflected the potential problems of building depreciation. The uncertainty existed, and still does exist, because traditional methods of valuing property do not incorporate an explicit allowance for the likely impact of building depreciation. The income received from an investment property is valued by reference to a single yield figure or capitalisation rate which reflects a host of variables, only one of which is depreciation. The concern is not that no allowance is made for depreciation, but rather that whatever allowance is made cannot be separately identified and then tested to see if it is adequate.

3. The building design professions were making more use of life cycle costing techniques. These allow the impact of building depreciation, amongst other things, to be incorporated within the framework for decision-making on building design and specification. If these techniques are to be effective, a knowledge of depreciation factors is required in order that accurate estimates may be made of the useful lives of buildings and building components.
4. It was apparent that in a very large number of cases the economic or functional life span of buildings was significantly shorter than the potential physical life span. This suggested a possible inefficiency in the use of physical resources.
5. The treatment of depreciation of assets in company accounts was standardised in the late 1970's by the issue of formal guidelines by the Accounting Standards Committee. The debate on these guidelines was dominated by the question of whether investment properties should be treated as a special case and granted exemption from the normal requirement to make provision for depreciation in the profit and loss account. The eventual decision to exempt investment properties from this requirement has been a matter of some controversy.

Objectives

The objectives of the CALUS research study were to examine the following main issues:

  i the current practice of investors and their advisers in taking depreciation into account in the acquisition, management and valuation of investment properties;
 ii the impact of building depreciation on property values;
iii the implications of research findings on building depreciation for property valuation and management practices; and
 iv the formulation of a method of investment appraisal which enables explicit allowance to be made for building depreciation.

Other matters also considered are as follows:

  v depreciation of land values;
 vi the role of the landlord and tenant relationship in depreciation;
vii building design, life cycle costing and depreciation;
viii the treatment of depreciation in company accounts;
 ix taxation and depreciation; and
  x the treatment of depreciation in overseas countries.

The focus of this book is points (i), (ii) and (iv). There is a considerable amount of empirical work in the CALUS report which examines these areas: the research method used and details of some of the findings are examined more fully in Chapter 5.

Perspectives of depreciation in the CALUS report

The CALUS report is a wide-ranging study of a subject hitherto poorly understood and not previously the subject of empirical research. It is therefore understandable that the report is not an in-depth focus upon a particular impact of commercial property depreciation, but rather that depreciation as a topic is viewed from several different perspectives. Those perspectives can be summarised as follows.

Building design

Chapter 8 of the CALUS report considers "Building Design and Life Cycle Costing". It states the three principal criteria for building design as aesthetic appearance, functional efficiency and costs-in-use, and describes the application of life cycle costing analysis as a means of reducing the total costs incurred over the life of a building. Life cycle costing is seen as a rational approach to minimising the costs of the physical deterioration of buildings whose success depends upon the ability to forecast both the physical and functional lives of buildings.

Property management

Chapter 7 ("The Role of the Landlord and Tenant Relationship in Depreciation") examines the manner in which the tenure of UK commercial buildings impacts upon the efficient management of those buildings, particularly the repair of deteriorating, obsolescent structures. The landlord and tenant relationship is seen as a potential constraint upon the ability of either party to efficiently counteract the impact of depreciation.

Accounting and taxation

The CALUS report describes current accounting regulations and undertakes a critical review of the accounting treatment of depreciation for investment properties. In addition, Chapter 9 of the CALUS report ("Tax and Depreciation") examines the peculiar UK practice of disallowing the depreciation of buildings as a cost which can be set against revenue for tax purposes, instead providing for capital allowances and annual writing down allowances on certain buildings in certain areas. The case for depreciation allowances is made, and in Chapter 11 a comparison is drawn with overseas systems of allowing building depreciation as a deduction against revenue for income taxes.

Valuation

"Property Valuation Methods" is the subject of Chapter 5 of the report and, as stated in the objectives of the study, is a major focus of the research. A distinction between the subjective assessment of investment worth and the objective test of market worth is drawn, and an appraisal technique is developed as a means of assessing investment worth and also as an aid to property valuation. (This technique is referred to in detail in Chapter 7.)

Investment

The CALUS report does not fully explore the implications of its findings upon property investment markets. There is no reference, for example, to the impact of depreciation upon conventional views of risk or the use of portfolio theory to diversify away the impact of depreciation in funds. There is however, some analysis of the pricing implications of the research findings, and investment considerations are paramount in Chapter 4 ("The Varying Impact of Depreciation for Different Types of Property") and Chapter 6 ("Analysis of Current Property Values").

These five areas are useful headings for a fuller survey of literature concerning depreciation. The literature review which follows uses such a scheme, but only briefly discusses works concerned primarily with building design, management, accounting and taxation, and valuation and pays fuller attention to investment considerations, which are central to this research. The survey ends at December 1987. There is little definitional consistency in these references, but no attempt is made at this stage to reconcile any such inconsistency. Appendix A to this book provides working definitions.

2. Other recent studies

Building design

Brown (1970) considered the impact of financial considerations upon the design of buildings and showed that the proposed life of a building, unless it is extremely short, will not have much effect upon the form of construction which would be employed. He shows that at most realistic discount rates it is not worth reducing construction costs if the building is to last more than a few years. This suggests that physical building life may be less of a depreciation factor than obsolescence. Salway (1986) confirms this. His research found that investors were unanimously of the view that most commercial buildings were likely to reach the end of their functional or economic lives well before they reached the end of their physical lives.

Stringer (1986) demonstrated how the legal framework constrains building design. Statute and case law can reduce flexibility of building design so that even if short-life buildings are financially rational and resource-efficient if may not be legally possible or advisable to construct them.

Many reports and articles published around 1986/87 concentrated upon the property and building design implications of the de-regulation of the City of London. Pepper and Morgan (1986), for example, refer to the need for more flexible offices, emphasise the need for higher quality buildings and describe the increased need for large uninterrupted dealing rooms and increased floor-to-ceiling heights. The implications of so-called *Big Bang* included an acceleration of obsolescence in City office buildings created by outdated design.

A survey of City of London occupier needs by Richard Ellis (Richard Ellis, 1985) provided justification for these findings, and indicated the increasing importance of building specification in accelerating the movements of occupiers within the City market, thereby impacting upon the investment returns to obsolete units.

Duffy (1986) describes the development of the city of the twentieth century around the prototype of the late nineteenth-century Chicago skyscraper. This was now an obsolete and misleading model when new requirements, all directly or indirectly derived from information technology, demanded a new kind of office building.

Povall (1986) is unequivocal in his opinion of the major cause of commercial building depreciation. He describes inflexibility as the key. This theme was repeated verbatim at a FIABCI conference in 1986 [1], in which John Worthington (DEGW) referred to service provision, floor-to-ceiling height, plan layout and building image as the four main concerns of City office tenants, all leading to the need for a flexible stock. Coates (1986) describes how "core and shell" approaches to property development improve building flexibility, which in turn "enhances lettability".

Healey and Baker undertook a national survey of office design in 1986-7. The report of this research (Healey and Baker, 1987) shows that design factors increasingly affected rental value. The report also ranked building design factors in order of importance. These were, in order:

---

1. See, for example, a report in Estates Times of July 1986 at page 11.

  i internal environmental control;
 ii heating system;
iii improved car parking;
 iv quality of internal finishes;
  v security;
 vi provision for cable trunking;
vii toilet facilities;
viii entrance hall;
 ix lift performance/reliability;
  x arrangements for kitchen/catering facilities; and
 xi external appearance of building.

This was a somewhat incomplete listing of building design factors (for example, plan layout of floors is absent) which nevertheless identified areas of potential obsolescence in office buildings.

Ferguson (1987) provides further details of expanding demands on office design emphasising the need for flexible flooring and quality internal environmental services. Coyne (1987) is sufficiently negative concerning all qualities of 1960's and 1970's office blocks to suggest demolition as the best solution.

Building design factors clearly impact upon obsolescence. A methodology for assessing the relationship and impact of these factors in a systematic way is developed in Chapter 4.

Property management

Speaking at the 1986 Building Industry Convention, Finn (1986) emphasised the increasing demand of tenants for frequent refurbishment of office space. Low inflation levels, over-supply of space and rapid developments in information technology had forced a change in tenant/owner relationships. In planning a renewal programme, he suggested it was essential to allow for low cost refurbishment every 5 to 10 years. The implications for property investors were, according to Finn, clear: property is a wasting investment unless frequent capital injection takes place, and the responsibility to carry out improvements and the leases which govern such responsibilities will have to change.

Coombes (1986) was more specific. Speaking at the CALUS Conference on Depreciation of Commercial Property, he expressed concern over the standard 25-year lease and the 1954 Landlord and Tenant Act, Part II and their combined impact upon the landlord and tenant relationship in a period of increasing impact of depreciation. It was no longer appropriate, he suggested, to have one standard lease length for all property types when the impact of depreciation and requirements for regular refurbishment arose at different intervals.

Shorter leases were required in all cases, but especially for industrial and office properties, where the impact of the 25-year lease was to leave a depreciating building unrefurbished as neither landlord nor tenant had the incentive to spend money on corrective measures.

To be specific, a building which requires refurbishment after 15 years but which is let subject to a 25-year lease will not easily be refurbished before year 25. From the tenant's point of view, while expenditure upon improvements should be allowed for in the agreement of a new rent at the start of a second lease, that compensation may not be adequate. The cost and management problems may additionally be excessive for a tenant whose main business is not investment in property, particularly if a move is envisaged at the end of the lease. From the landlord's point of view, upwards-only rent review clauses protect the landlord's income from even a rapidly depreciating office building, reducing his incentive to refurbish. In addition, the Landlord and Tenant Acts may actually prevent his gaining access to the building to carry out the necessary work before the end of the lease.

At the 1986 Office Agents Society/Chartered Surveyor Weekly conference [2] conventional leasing terms were heavily criticised, and the effect of this perceived difficulty in a market of functionally obsolete office buildings was to draw many of the speakers to the conclusion that the best option for office tenants was owner occupation. This is a severe indictment of the legal environment within which the landlord and tenant relationship operates, engendered primarily as a result of building depreciation.

Accounting and taxation

Introduction

The lack of attention paid by the UK property profession to the subject of depreciation is in extreme contrast to the depth of tradition which characterises the treatment of the topic by accountants. Chapter 10 of the CALUS report ("The Treatment of Depreciation in Company Accounts") opens with a 1903 quotation which establishes this tradition:

> The question of depreciation is one upon which so many articles have been written, and so many opinions expressed, that there would not appear to be much more which could profitably be said on the subject. (Armstrong, 1903)

---

2. *Reported in CSW of 30 October 1986 at page 449.*

Depreciation is therefore a fundamental concept within accounting practice. This flows in the UK from the principle underlying accounting, which is the *accruals* basis. A company's cash flow is measured and realised within discrete time periods, but this may not give a true and fair picture of its profitability. For example, heavy expenditure on research and development of products may appear to reduce profits or create losses for a considerable period before benefits are realised. In accounts, therefore, such expenditure may sometimes be rolled-up and carried forward (accrued) until the year(s) in which benefits are realised. There are several standard means of calculating this charge.

Methods of depreciation

The most common method or basis of depreciation, used by over 80% of major companies (Holmes and Sugden, 1987), is the straight line (or fixed instalment) method. Several other methods are also employed. The following discussion of depreciation methods relies heavily on Holmes and Sugden, 1986, whose views of the relative worth of these methods are summarised below.

The straight line or fixed instalment method

Depreciation under the fixed instalment method is computed as follows:

$$\text{Annual depreciation} = \frac{\text{Cost} - \text{residual value}}{\text{Expected useful life}}$$

The straight line method is ideal where the service provided by the asset continues unabated throughout its useful life, as might be the case with a 21-year lease of a building; and it is generally used wherever the equal allocation of cost provides a reasonably fair measure of the asset's service, for example, for buildings, plant, machinery, equipment, vehicles and patents.

The declining balance or reducing balance method

The declining balance method used to be the most popular method of depreciation, but it has largely been supplanted in recent years by the straight line method. Under the declining balance method, the annual depreciation charge represents a fixed percentage of the net book value cost less aggregate depreciation.

$$\text{Depreciation rate} = 1 - n \sqrt{\frac{\text{Residual value}}{\text{Cost}}}$$

(as a decimal)

where n = useful life in years

Among the disadvantages of the declining balance method are:

i most users do not calculate the rate appropriate to each particular item of plant, but use standard percentages, which tend to be too low rather than too high;

ii unless notional adjustments are made to cost and residual value, it is impossible to calculate satisfactorily a declining balance rate if the residual value is nil; and

iii even if the asset is assigned a nominal scrap value, or if there is some residual value but it is small in relation to cost, the method is unlikely to be satisfactory without notional adjustments, because it leads to such high charges in the early years.

The sum of the years' digits method

The sum of the (years') digits method is not commonly found in the UK, though it is used as a method of allowing accelerated depreciation in the United States (where accounting depreciation, provided it is computed by an acceptable method, is also used for tax purposes). It is occasionally found in the UK in connection with activities like leasing which involve heavy outlays in early years.

In this method, the cost less any residual value is divided by the sum of the years' digits to give what may be termed a unit of depreciation. In the last year of expected life, one unit of depreciation is provided; in the next to last, two; in the one before that, three; and so on. The sum of the years' digits is simply the sum of the series: $(1 + 2 + 3 + 4 \ldots + n)$, where n represents the expected life of the asset.

The formula for computing the sum of the digits is $n(n + 1)/2$, where n is the number of years. Thus, to apply the sum of the digits to an asset having a life of 5 years, the divisor (the sum of the years' digits) is $5(5 + 1)/2 = 15$, and the first year's depreciation is 5/15ths of (cost minus residual value), the second year's 4/15ths, and so on.

The production unit method

In this method, depreciation is charged according to the number of units produced in the period.

$$\text{Charge per unit} = \frac{\text{Cost of residual value}}{\substack{\text{Estimated number of units} \\ \text{to be produced during the} \\ \text{asset's effective lifetime}}}$$

This method can be used only where all the units an asset produces are identical or involve the same *work value*. It makes costing of machine costs simple; and has the result of charging high depreciation where a machine is being used round the clock (which is not unreasonable). It can however be very misleading in that there is no charge for depreciation if the machine lies idle. Clearly an unused asset still depreciates with the lapse of time, and the idleness of a machine may indicate an earlier than estimated end to its useful life.

The annuity method

The annuity method is sometimes used for the amortisation of leasehold properties, that is to write off the premium (the initial cost of the lease) over the term of the lease.

The annual depreciation charge under the annuity method is calculated by dividing the cost of the asset (less the present value of any expected residual value) by the present value of an annuity of £1 per annum for the estimated life of the asset.

The sinking fund method

The sinking fund method is similar to the concept of a sinking fund to provide for the repayment of a loan. A given sum of money is invested each year outside the business sufficient to provide, with interest, the amount of money required to replace the asset at the end of its useful life. The method is rarely used, for two main reasons:

i   the cost of replacement is unlikely to be known with any accuracy when the asset is originally acquired; and

ii   most businesses have opportunities for investment within the business which will yield far more than is usually available from fixed-interest stocks, in which sinking funds are normally invested.

There are exceptions to the general requirement for a depreciation allowance. Companies may disregard the requirements for depreciation allowances set out under the Companies Act 1985 if by doing so they would provide a better or more "true and fair" view of the financial affairs of the company.

Exceptions to common depreciation practice

The most significant exception to normal depreciation practice is freehold property. Statement of Standard Accounting Practice (SSAP) 12 (Accounting for Depreciation) states that freehold land will not normally require a provision for depreciation. On the other hand, the buildings which stand on freehold land should, under the requirements of SSAP 12, be depreciated:

> Buildings have a limited life which may be materially affected by technological and environmental changes and they should be depreciated...

However, generally rising prices create considerable difficulties. Accounts continue to be based on historic costs. Inflation therefore produces a series of anomalies, not least of which is the requirement to depreciate freehold buildings which form part of properties which are annually revalued, usually upwards in a period of inflation. This problem resulted in SSAP 19 (Accounting for Investment Properties), which allows that investment properties, other than leaseholds with 20 years or less unexpired, should not be depreciated (Accounting Standards Committee, 1981).

SSAP 19 is not uncontroversial. It leads to a potential over-statement of profit as the need to refurbish is effectively rolled-up, and it leads to relative errors where companies are excessively exposed to depreciating office and industrial buildings. Bowie (1982) was clearly critical of accounting standards and added greatly to the increasing awareness of depreciation referred to above:

> Depreciation is too important to be ignored. Owners of property, whether for occupation or investment, should understand that buildings <u>do</u> wear out, and the capital invested in them is eroded. If it is correct for an owner occupier to provide for depreciation in his accounts, then the owner of an identical property let to a third party on full repairing terms must recognise that if he chooses to make no provision for depreciation then any full distributions of rental income must include an element for depreciation. The lessee is not responsible, apart from maintenance, so the depreciation must be within the rent paid to the owner...

He continues:

> There is a curious anomaly in SSAP 19. It states that leaseholds
> with 20 years or less unexpired life must be depreciated out of the
> account. Logically this should also apply to any building which has
> an *economic useful life* of 20 years or less – but no one seems to have
> thought of that one. It would be difficult to swap or amend SSAP
> 19 in the near future so is there anything that should be done? I
> suggest that even more information about the make-up of the
> property investment portfolio should now be published.

Little published material develops Bowie's criticisms. The CALUS
report is one of few later critical references to the subject area. The
importance of depreciation of property to accounting is that increased
concern and possibly increased incidence will begin to undermine
confidence in published accounts and consequently in the pricing of
property sector shares.

The UK taxation treatment of depreciation is also generally regarded as problematic, especially in comparison with overseas. Dew
(1986) confirmed that of 22 countries in which Sun Alliance operates,
depreciation is required as a tax allowance in 21. The UK is the
exception.

The focus of attention has clearly shifted in recent years from these
relatively clear problems of general accounting practice in its applications to property to the importance of depreciation as a factor in the
valuation and performance of property investments.

Valuation

The CALUS report describes methods of incorporating depreciation
objectively within DCF-based appraisals of property. Such appraisals
are stated to have two uses:

 i for the subjective analysis of investment worth; and
 ii as an aid to property valuation.

It is clear, however, that market valuations are the product of wholly
different requirements to analyses of investment worth (see, for
example, Baum and Crosby, 1988). The former is based upon an
observation and prediction of market behaviour. If depreciation is
ignored by a market then it is arguable that a prediction of the most
likely selling price, that is a market valuation, will also ignore it. Direct
capital comparison is the most likely technique to be adopted.
Investment appraisal, on the other hand, is likely to be based upon the
discounting of the future costs and benefits and it is crucial to such an

exercise that depreciation is taken fully into account. Arguably, therefore, depreciation-sensitive appraisal methods are of use in appraisal but are of little or no use in valuation, even as a check.

Depreciation is, however, directly relevant in valuing certain properties which are rarely sold, for balance sheet, rating and other purposes. The depreciated replacement cost basis requires the valuer to assess the market value of the land in its existing use, to add the replacement cost of the building and to adjust that cost for economic and functional obsolescence and for environmental factors. These three factors are specifically referred to in the guidelines prepared by Asset Valuation Standards Committee of the RICS (RICS, 1988), from which the following extract is taken:

Deductions will normally be made under three main headings.

Economic obsolescence – the age and condition of the existing building and the probable cost of future maintenance as compared with that of a modern building.

Functional obsolescence – suitability for the present use and the prospect of its continuance or use for some other purposes by the business.

Environmental factors – existing uses should be considered in relation to the surrounding area and local and national planning policies.

(A fuller definitional study is undertaken in Chapter 4.)

Clarke (1986) suggests that the valuer is often less well placed than his client to comment upon functional obsolescence, implying a concealed difficulty in the client/advisor relationship and a need for the property profession to learn more about depreciation and obsolescence. Clarke also suggests an increase in this difficulty caused by accelerating change.

Cherry (1986) refers to the effect of depreciation on investment valuations, again failing to distinguish clearly between the requirements of a valuation and an appraisal. He does, however, repeat concerns regarding the uncertainty of the profession, especially regarding the identification of building depreciation, in its valuation role.

There is clearly a need for greater understanding of the sources and impact of depreciation for valuations undertaken on a depreciated replacement cost basis. The wider problems of market valuations which ignore depreciation as an explicit item are more correctly identified as the problems which investors suffer in the identification of good and bad buys. These are considered in full in Chapter 8. The considerable quantity of recent literature which refers directly or obliquely to the impact of depreciation upon property investment appraisal and property investment performance is dealt with immediately below.

Investment

The impact of depreciation

In a seminal paper, Bowie (1982) calculated that the effect of depreciation upon the average income yield from a portfolio equally split between offices, shops, and industrials was, given certain assumptions, to reduce it from 5.3% to 4.2%: "in other words, one fifth of the income would need to be set aside for depreciation".

This paper is often identified as the beginning of a serious interest by property professionals in property investment depreciation. The CALUS report (Salway, 1986) introduction is absolutely explicit:

The idea for this study first arose some five years ago. That it did arise is due in large measure to the comments and articles of Mr Norman Bowie. He calculated what many of us felt at the time, that the property market might not be pricing property for the effects of depreciation. . .

Bowie's impact is arguably not limited to an arousal of professional interest. The performance of property types identified by Bowie as particularly prone to the impact of depreciation performed very badly over the period 1982 - 1987, and this was largely the result of yield changes (a proxy for the attitude of investors) rather than poor rental value growth.

Tables 5 and 6 show the relative performance of average yields and rents for hypothetical prime property (that is, property unaffected by depreciation) over the period May 1980 to May 1987. While rents rose consistently in all sectors, yields also rose on average.

Table 5: Average yields, 1980-1987

	1980	1981	1982	1983	1984	1985	1986	1987
Shops	4.8	4.7	4.7	5.0	4.8	4.8	5.1	5.3
Offices	5.2	5.2	5.4	6.0	6.3	6.8	7.4	7.6
Industrials	6.9	6.9	7.2	8.4	9.2	10.2	10.6	10.5

Source: Investors Chronicle Hillier Parker (1988)

Table 6: Rental values, 1980-1987

ICHP Rent Index	1980	1981	1982	1983	1984	1985	1986	1987
Shops	170	181	195	203	219	244	273	328
Offices	145	164	177	183	191	208	227	272
Industrials	156	164	169	171	175	181	193	203

Source: Investors Chronicle Hillier Parker (1988)
Note: Index is of values for prime property

Tables 7 and 8 show the impact of these combined figures on capital values and rates of return respectively and show the very poor yield-driven performance of property over the period 1982 to 1987. 1983 in particular was a very bad year for performance, with only shops showing a positive return (Table 8). A more pertinent revelation is the performance of the depreciation-prone office and industrial sectors.

Bowie (1982) had shown how the impact of depreciation should be much greater, *a priori*, in these sectors. Table 9 shows his hypothesised running or income yields for prime investments and the true net yield after allowances for building depreciation have been taken out of income.

The greatest impact is on industrials, then offices, with shops considerably less affected. Table 7 shows exactly this. The ICHP index for May 1982 demonstrated marginally reduced capital growth for shops, but greatly reduced growth for offices and a capital **loss** for industrials. The average growth (loss) of value of shops, offices and industrials for the period 1982-1986 was 7.22%, (0.72%) and (4.76%) respectively, at a time when inflation averaged 5.62%, the growth in the value of gilts averaged 7.02% and the growth in the value of equities averaged 20.06% per annum.

Table 7: Capital values, 1980-1987 (% change over year)

	1980	1981	1982	1983	1984	1985	1986	1987
Shops	16.7	10.1	8.0	-1.4	13.3	11.9	4.3	13.5
Offices	15.7	13.3	2.5	-6.2	0.1	-0.3	0.3	9.2
Industrials	18.8	5.5	-1.0	-10.2	-9.5	-6.5	3.4	5.8

Source: Investors Chronicle Hillier Parker (1988)

Table 8: Rates of return, 1980-87 (% change over year)

	1980	1981	1982	1983	1984	1985	1986	1987
Shops	21.9	15.2	12.9	3.5	18.5	17.0	9.3	19.0
Offices	21.3	18.8	7.8	-0.6	6.3	6.4	7.3	17.1
Industrials	26.5	12.7	6.1	-3.0	-1.3	3.1	14.2	16.9

Source: Investors Chronicle Hillier Parker (1988)

Table 9: The impact of depreciation on running yields (%)

	Running yield	True yield	Reduction
Shops	3.50	3.25	7.14
Offices	5.00	3.90	22.00
Industrials	7.50	5.50	26.67

Source: Bowie (1982)

Thus, although property suffered an arguably cyclical trough of performance between 1982 and 1986, the performance of the relatively depreciation-free retail sector, with good real returns (averaging 6.62% per annum) compared with the performance of the depreciation-prone office and industrial sectors (averaging (0.18%) and (1.8%) per annum respectively) demonstrates a highly differential effect, which justifies the comments of Bowie to such an extent that it is not inconceivable that his 1982 paper influenced the attitudes of investors and resulted in a major revision of the pricing of these sectors.

It is probable that there was an element of over-correction in these performance figures. Bowie, in a later paper (1983a), was quick to point out that "depreciation is not well understood. . . there is much to be done". The CALUS report was the first significant response to his paper, appearing when the performance of the property market was about to turn upwards, making it difficult to judge how accurate the initial reaction had been, and how efficient the property market of the early- to mid-1980's was. There is little doubt, however, that Bowie's 1982 paper contributed significantly to efficient pricing and created a market eager for information about depreciation.

The effect of depreciation on office investments in particular was the subject of several conferences and publications in 1985 and 1986. Wilson (1985), contributing to a book on office development, argued that the impact of depreciation on value was sensitive to the relative cost of depreciating *assets* within buildings, so that depreciation became much more noticeable in a period of stagnant property values and rising costs (for example, 1983). Wilson also referred to the impact of depreciation often being hidden by the willingness of tenants to carry out major improvement works, even though they were not required by the lease terms to do so. (This is a factor which is referred to specifically in Chapter 5.)

The 1986 CALUS conference (Depreciation of Commercial Property) included two papers (Dew, 1986 and Hallett, 1986) which referred to the investment, appraisal and property performance considerations created by depreciation and prompted a very full review in *Estates Times* ("Commentary, Depreciation: a Risk Exposed" and "Valuation Methods Come Under Attack", September 26 1986, pages 8 and 11). Dew referred to an increase in rates of obsolescence: this is examined further in Chapter 6. He suggested that sectors of the property market had been overpriced, repeating Bowie (1982).

Hallett was more pointed in his views. Given that office investments had shown only 0.5% real returns since 1945 and taking illiquidity and depreciation into effect, his opinion was that prime offices, then selling at 5% yields, should not be bought at any yield below 7.5%. The implication of this statement was that he considered prime offices to be 50% overpriced. Old buildings, he added, were better buys, because depreciation had run its course, yet yields were higher. This is examined in Chapters 6 and 7. Hallett also predicted accelerating depreciation.

Fraser (1986) constructed an argument, *a priori*, for explaining the relative impact of obsolescence (as he termed the effect on value) and used a comparison of two property indices to estimate a value for depreciation of industrial property. He defined obsolescence as "the annual rate by which the value growth of the individual property lags behind that of equivalent, currently modern, property". Going on to suggest that historic obsolescence of investment property in the UK has not been accurately measured and that future obsolescence is difficult to predict, he hypothesised, like Bowie, that offices and industrials could suffer greater annual depreciation than agricultural and prime shop investments, simply because the majority of the value of the latter is protected by the value of the land element of the property. He estimated an annual rate of office depreciation at 2% per annum assuming a 60-year life, or 3.9% assuming a 30-year life.

His major contribution to the debate was, however, a comparison of the Investors Chronicle Hillier Parker Industrial Rent Index and the Jones Lang Wootton equivalent. The latter had produced average returns of 2% per annum below inflation and 2% per annum below the former. This, argued Fraser, is explained by the construction of the two indices. Whereas the ICHP index abstracts from actual property performance by measuring the rental value of continually modern property on a fixed site, the JLW index measures the rental value of a consistent portfolio of actual properties. The ICHP index suffers no depreciation; the JLW index does. Hence industrial "depreciation through obsolescence" runs at around 2% per annum. (This analysis ignores changes in yields: see Chapters 5 and 6.)

Richard Ellis, in the April 1987 Quarterly Property Investment Bulletin (Richard Ellis, 1987) concentrated upon office investment outside central London. It reported a "radical change" in the approach of the institutional investment market to offices. Investors had showed little interest in the sector and substantial "adjustments" (increases) in yields had taken place over the previous two years. Investors had attempted to sell older office buildings. Richard Ellis examined the reasons for this, concluding that:

> . . .physical depreciation remains probably the most significant of all the causes of declining value, which is only now being fully recognised.

The report identified contributing causes of depreciation, as follows: deterioration of the fabric, aesthetic obsolescence, functional obsolescence, inflexible configuration and rising service charges.

As a result of these factors, provincial offices, with particularly low site values as a percentage of the whole property value, had shown a 9% capital loss over the year 1986 to 1987, evidence of a market becoming more specific and efficient in its judgement of the impact of depreciation in a period of sudden performance upturn (see Table 8) after 5 poor years. Capital values of all offices in the ICHP index increased by 9% in the year May 1986 to May 1987 (see Table 7); Richard Ellis suggest a 27% gain in value of City offices, a 2% gain in value of Greater London offices and a loss of 9% in the value of offices in the provinces over a similar period, explained primarily by the differential impact of obsolescence.

A comment by Edward Erdman (1987) provides a contrast to this. Examining the views of tenants of industrial space with the assistance of the CBI, they state:

> . . .changing commercial markets are likely to be the main reason behind building stock reassessment, followed by technological advance and company expansion. Specific property problems, obsolescence for example, are felt to be less important.

Given that Richard Ellis (1987) and the CALUS report, among several others, are clear that technological advance is a primary cause of functional obsolescence, this suggests that depreciation was still not, despite Richard Ellis' hope, "being fully recognised".

This report marks the end of the period covering the empirical work described in the following chapters. Depreciation, it is clear, impacted upon office (particularly provincial) and industrial markets considerably between 1982 and 1987. The effects were initially felt widely, and only later is there evidence that differential effects distinguishing depreciation-prone and depreciation-sensitive sectors were being observed. It is clear, however, that little had been discovered about the precise sources of depreciation, their relative importance and their combined impact upon performance and pricing.

Techniques for the measurement and analysis of depreciation

At the same time that the impact of depreciation was being felt in markets, techniques for its measurement and analysis were being developed. Fraser's work (1986) is referred to above: it suggested a 2% depreciation rate for industrials by measuring the divergence between depreciation-free and depreciation-prone indices. This was not, however, the first reference.

Blandon and Ward (1978) produced work which concluded that the profitability of property investment depended upon the probability that inflation will in the long term be higher than the rate implicit in current valuations. This conclusion was arrived at by comparing property investment and gilt investment. A vital distinguishing factor which was stripped out of property performance in the course of this analysis was property depreciation. It was shown that implied growth rates on new prime property, arrived at by a comparison of redemption yields on gilts and initial yields on property, considerably understate the growth in rents which is implied for new property because the rent will rise by a lesser amount than that of a continually new building (see Chapter 2).

Where: g is the implied rental growth for a continually new building;
        a is the implied rental growth for an actual property; and
        d is the compound rate by which the rents on older properties fall short of the rents on new property,

Blandon and Ward derive the relationship

$$a = g - d - dg$$

However, as they state:

. . .to convert this formula to practical use an estimate of the *depreciation* of rental levels (based) on the age of property is needed. Here the paucity of data available is even worse than that usually characteristic of the property sector.

They overcome this problem by using a report of the Economic Advisory Group (1974), which provides estimates of rents for new and old office accommodation as shown in Table 10.

The results, based apparently on a cross-section analysis disaggregated by sub-location, show annual rental depreciation varying (depending on sector and assumptions regarding age) from 1.51% to 4.03% per annum. This is a rare, albeit incomplete, assessment of average rental depreciation, which leads Blandon and Ward to take an average rate of depreciation, for illustration purposes, of 2% per annum, allowing them to draw a conclusion about the actual rate of rental growth required on a 6.75% building. At a time when undated gilts yielded 15%, that was a required growth of 13.2%, to be compared with an apparent implied growth of a continually new building of only 10.9%.

Table 10: Rental depreciation rate in the City, 1973 (%)

Area of the City	Rents on *new* accommodation	Rents on *old* accommodation	Dep'n rate with assumed age		
	£/sq ft	£/sq ft	25 yrs	30 yrs	35 yrs
Insurance	18.00	7.50	3.56	2.96	2.53
Shipping and commodity markets	17.50	7.00	3.73	3.10	2.65
Smithfield and Billingsgate	7.00	3.50	2.81	2.33	2.00
Fleet Street	11.00	6.50	2.13	1.77	1.51
Bank	21.50	8.00	4.03	3.35	2.86

Source: Economic Advisory Group (1974)

In papers published around the mid-1980's, Sykes (1984a, 1984b and 1986) adopted a different model for analysing the impact of depreciation. (This work was also the basis of comments made by Wilson (1985).) Unlike Blandon and Ward, who suggested a measure of depreciation based on the compound rate by which the rents on older properties fall short of the rents on new property, Sykes related depreciation wholly to deterioration, and hypothesised that such depreciation was wholly curable by the periodic injection of refurbishment expenditure on the building. Given knowledge about:

    i the target rate of return (for example, the gilt rate, risk-adjusted if necessary);
    ii the initial property yield;
    iii refurbishment costs as a percentage of the open market value following refurbishment; and
    iv the periodicity of refurbishment works,

it is possible, using Sykes' model, to calculate the implied rate of rental growth needed to make the subject property a competitive purchase proposition (see Table 11). In terms of output, this is directly analogous to the work of Blandon and Ward. The definition or proxy of depreciation is, however, fundamentally different and comparatively flawed. It is presumed that depreciation can be wholly cured by expenditure, a proposition which is counter-intuitive (and is examined fully in Chapter 6 and 7). (Brown (1986) produces further criticisms of Sykes' model; see below.)

Table 11: Refurbishment and required rental growth (% per annum)

Refurbishment costs (%)	Refurbishment period		
	= 15 years	= 20 years	= 25 years
0	6.67	6.67	6.67
5	6.95	6.85	6.80
10	7.24	7.04	6.92
15	7.55	7.24	7.06
20	7.88	7.45	7.20
25	8.22	7.67	7.35
30	8.58	7.90	7.50
35	8.97	8.14	7.67
40	9.38	8.39	7.84
45	9.83	8.67	8.01
50	10.30	8.95	8.20

Source: Sykes (1984b)
Notes: 1. Target rate 12%
         2. Initial yield 6% (with 5-yearly rent reviews)

A report by Debenham, Tewson and Chinnocks (1985) supports this latter criticism by referring to "irremedial (sic) obsolescence". This paper refers to "a clear need for the profession to address. . . (the effect of obsolescence on valuations) so that a more practical approach can be introduced", but suffers from a critical lack of definitional clarity, especially in failing to make the necessary distinction between a valuation and an appraisal. Assuming it is the latter which is the subject under consideration, the paper accepts that market pricing makes an allowance for obsolescence in variations in yields and rental values between new and ageing buildings, but in a non-rigorous manner. By implication, a more scientific approach may lead to better informed buy/sell decisions.

Adopting an approach similar to that of Sykes, the contribution of this work is the recognition that the relative proportions of land and building value in the total property will affect the rate of depreciation as provided by the annual equivalent of necessary remedial expenditure. Thus the rate of depreciation of a City office building, utilising assumed values for relevant variables, might be half as great as the equivalent rate of depreciation of a similar Hereford office building.

Fraser (1986) constructed a model of initial yield determination for property which is very similar to the model proposed by Blandon and Ward. He repeats the same basic point, that property prices and yields should reflect expected obsolescence and that the implied rental growth expectation should incorporate the effect on growth of the market's expected rate of depreciation from obsolescence. Surprisingly, however, in a paper which attempts in a particularly radical manner to identify the reasons driving yield differentials between gilts, equities and property, Fraser does not support the conclusion reached above, namely that depreciation perceptions were heightened around 1982, and that consequent poor property performance can be related to this. Fraser's explanation is as follows:

...the yield model is no more than a statement of a basic condition for rational investment. It indicates that property yields will tend towards the level required to provide investors with the same total return as is expected from a close substitute investment, with appropriate allowance made for differences in risk and other investment qualities. Any suggestion that the yield model is invalid implies that the insurance companies and pension funds which dominate the market are not striving to achieve the most beneficial combination of risk and return.

It is contended that the behaviour of property yields since 1979 reflects substantial movements in the differential between gilt yields and property's target return. With little change likely to have occurred in the relative liquidity, marketability, transaction costs, management costs and taxation liability of the two investments, such movements would indicate important changes in the institutions' perception of property's risk relative to gilts over this period.

Fraser then examines trends in yield relationships between 1979 and 1981 and between 1982 and 1985. In the latter period, yields (see Table 3.2) rose: and "clearly, such trends indicate a rise in property's target return relative to gilt yields, this differential being largely a function of the relative risk of the two investments as perceived by the dominant investors". It seems clear from the analysis presented above that fears of depreciation may be a primary cause of the rise in perceptions of property's relative risk over that period. Unfortunately, there is no attempt to estimate or measure its impact in the Fraser model.

Finally, Brown (1986) attempts a model which can be tested empirically and which analyses the problem of obsolescence and its impact on valuations. In doing so, he first questions Sykes' refurbishment model (Sykes, 1984) as being unsound in economics terms, implying as it does that refurbishment has no impact upon the selling yield of a property and that yields remain constant as a building ages. His own analysis is based on the hypothesis that valuers are correctly assessing underlying growth prospects (and, by implication, the future impact of depreciation and obsolescence) if realised growth in a property is statistically indistinguishable from expected growth on average (in other words, realised growth should fluctuate randomly round its expected value). His analysis uses the capital asset pricing model to show that industrials had been overpriced over the analysis period (that is, they had experienced negative abnormal growth which might be the product of underestimated depreciation) while shops had been underpriced and offices were fairly priced. When combined in a portfolio in the right proportion and with hindsight, it was "possible to diversify away many of the problems associated with obsolescence".

Brown concludes from his analysis that it is difficult to justify the belief that property values do not take into consideration the effects of obsolescence. However, he admits to the limitations of his extreme technique. For example, it is based on seven observations when "it would need to be shown that there is a significant difference between realised growth and expected growth and that this difference is maintained over long periods". Consequently, he limits his conclusions to there being a lack of proof for the negative: that is, it is not possible from this study to say that yields are always in error.

Brown's analysis is further and more critically flawed by his use of the capital asset pricing model, relying as it does on use of the historic volatility of property returns against a market index, measured by beta, as a source of the risk premium. It is only this assumption which permits the estimation of growth expectations in the market. Assumptions underlying the capital asset pricing model are questionable in a property market context, but (more problematically) it is probable that relative risk measures are incorrect for the three sectors. Historic volatility is a dubious proxy for property risk given the use of valuations in indices and a lack of trading. Valuation smoothing is of greater effect where market activity is low. Where market activity levels vary between the sectors under comparison (as they certainly do), errors in beta result even if the analytical foundation is sound. For further criticism of this approach, see Baum (1989b).

Brown's analysis is inconclusive. There is some evidence that the investment market takes depreciation into account, but whether it does so correctly it is impossible to say.

3. Summary

While there is some confusion over terminology (depreciation and obsolescence are often used as if interchangeable) it is clear that depreciation has several recognized and major impacts upon property. These include building design, property management, accounting and taxation, valuation and investment. It is the last of these which is the focus of attention of this research. Recent work has been carried out (in addition to the CALUS report) which has examined or implied an examination of the impact of depreciation on investment performance. Estimates of around 2% per annum in loss of return are not untypical.

Other work has concentrated on producing techniques for its measurement or analysis, and ranges from refurbishment models flawed by assumptions of total curability of obsolescence, by the use of capital asset pricing model, by inadequate model development or by inadequate empirical analysis.

The CALUS study produced the fullest empirical study to date of the effect of depreciation on rental value. For this reason, the methodology of this research is developed from that basis, which is fully discussed in Chapter 5.

An approach is needed which combines a clear definitional framework, knowledge of the impact of depreciation based on empirical analysis and an analytical framework which models the investment cash flow and investors' behaviour realistically. Chapter 4 establishes definitions and a taxonomy of depreciation. Chapters 6 and 7 attempt the empirical analysis, while Chapter 8 develops a decision model. Each relies on the foundation supplied by the CALUS report, which remains the major advance from Bowie's initial exploration in 1982.

Chapter 4

A classification of property investment depreciation and obsolescence

1. Depreciation and obsolescence

The literature review described in Chapter 3 is dominated by non-academic and non-theoretical references to depreciation and obsolescence. There is no discernible development in UK works of a body of knowledge and theory which defines and classifies these twin concepts, outside the mass of literature in accounting which concentrates upon the techniques used in the application of depreciation to profit and loss accounts, and a partial definition embodied in the RICS Asset Valuation Standards Committee guidelines (see Chapter 3).

In North America, on the other hand, the impact of depreciation upon investment return has for many years been very great as a result of two factors. First, accelerated depreciation allowances against income taxation have until recently differentiated property investment from other investment vehicles and raised consciousness of depreciation among real estate academics and professional practitioners. Second, the standard three values approach to appraisal in North America has meant that the cost approach is used much more in property valuation than it is in the UK, and depreciation is an important element in that approach (see Chapter 3).

Considerable confusion surrounds the use and definition of the two terms, depreciation and obsolescence, in UK references. An early example of UK definitions is provided by Chapman (1973) who defines depreciation as a "fall in value, hence, in accounting depreciation is the reduction in the value of an asset through wear and tear or obsolesence"; the latter term is "the drop in value of an asset which has passed its peak of use or productivity". This is helpful, but the clarity of definitions appears to have retarded since then. The two terms are sometimes used interchangeably (for example, Debenham, Tewson and Chinnocks, 1985; see Chapter 3) and usually without precision. In North American real estate texts, however, there are invariably attempts to establish a simple definition and classification of depreciation, the generic term, and obsolescence, a contributing factor.

Wofford (1983) defines depreciation and categorises its three sources as physical deterioration, functional obsolescence and economic or locational obsolescence:

> **Depreciation**, as used in appraisal, is the loss in value from any cause. The sources of depreciation may be categorised into three classifications: physical deterioration, functional obsolescence, and economic obsolescence. **Physical deterioration** is the loss in value due to the actual *wearing out* of the improvements. **Functional obsolescence** is the inability of an improvement to perform the job for which it is designed. For instance, the increased use of computer equipment calls for office buildings with adequate air conditioning and floors strong enough to support the weight of the machines. Buildings built several years ago that do not have these capabilities suffer from depreciation from functional obsolescence.... **Economic obsolescence**, also called **locational obsolescence**, is the loss in value due to factors outside the property itself. For example, the deterioration of a neighbourhood may reduce the value of a home. Likewise, changes in traffic patterns may reduce the value of a retail store. . .

Wurtzebach and Miles (1984) follow a similar structure, but produce a more detailed definition and classification. First, their definition is more specific:

> The concept of depreciation is pervasive in real estate. It is meant here as an appraisal or valuation concept, and it is met again in later chapters as an accounting concept and then as a tax concept. As used here, **depreciation** refers to reduction in the value of buildings or improvements as a result of physical, functional or economic factors.

Second, they split physical depreciation (not deterioration) into curable and incurable elements:

Physical depreciation may either be **curable** or **incurable**. Curable physical depreciation is also known as **deferred maintenance**, because the primary cause of such depreciation is the failure of the owner to maintain the property on an ongoing basis. Such depreciation is called **curable depreciation** because the cost of eliminating or correcting it is less than or equal to the value that will be added to the property as a result. Most items of *normal* maintenance come under this heading.

Examples of curable physical depreciation include replacing broken windows, painting the exterior and interior of a house, and cleaning and making minor replacements to the furnace. In all of these cases, the cost to cure is relatively small and is undoubtedly justified (in an economic sense).

The other type of physical depreciation is that which is incurable. The term **incurable** does not refer to the impossibility of curing the defect, since virtually any physical defect can be repaired or replaced, but to the lack of economic justification in doing so. Physical depreciation is considered *incurable depreciation* if the cost to cure or correct the physical defect is greater than the value that will be added to the property as a result.

Their distinction between curable and incurable depreciation is based on an economic test. Incurable depreciation must also include apparent physical impossibilities (increasing slab-to-slab height, for example) but, as it is usually possible to demolish and rebuild, an economic test is probably all that is needed, and for that reason it is adopted within this book.

They also suggest that the terms functional obsolescence and functional depreciation are interchangeable (and that such a factor may again be curable or incurable) and that economic or locational depreciation is an alternative for economic obsolescence. This is less helpful.

Shenkel (1984) uses the terms physical depreciation, functional obsolescence and economic obsolescence, and confirms a (to date in this introduction) missing detail:

Economic depreciation also is not curable. The examples (in the text) refer to environmental or neighbourhood factors that reduce a dwelling's value. Economic depreciation is not curable since it is difficult to remove these deficiencies by modernisation or rehabilitation of the property appraised.

The rare UK attempts at definition (for example, Bowie (1982)) appear to be straightforwardly derivative of the mainstream North American literature. There are, however, exceptions. For example, Fraser (1984) uses the term "economic obsolescence" to explain under-utilisation of a site (see below). The RICS Asset Valuation Standards Committee guidelines (RICS, 1988), on the other hand, define economic obsolescence as "the age and condition of the existing building and the probable cost of future maintenance as compared with that of a modern building", which appears close to the North American definition of physical depreciation. The RICS definition of functional obsolescence – "suitability for the present use and the prospect of its continuance or use for some other purposes by the business" – is much closer to Wofford's definition, while Shenkel's definition of economic depreciation is also close to the RICS term "environmental factors" ("existing uses should be considered in relation to the surrounding area and local and national planning policies"), although this does introduce, like Fraser, the effect of planning policy into the classification.

In conclusion, there is a considerable degree of confusion surrounding definitions of depreciation and obsolescence. Given the superior level of development of the North American classification and the lack of a consistent UK alternative, it is the North American system which provides the best starting point. In confirming this view by implication, Salway (1986) follows a similar, but more detailed, system of classification in the CALUS report (see below).

Depreciation and obsolescence: definitions

Basic definitions are an essential prerequisite not only to an understanding of the subject under examination but also to the construction of a model for its analysis. A full list of definitions is provided in Appendix A. The following basic definitions are derived from the North American school and an accounting definition of obsolescence in Baxter (1981), similar to that used in Salway (1986). They clearly distinguish depreciation as the effect, and obsolescence as the cause.

Depreciation is a loss in the real existing use value of property.

Obsolescence is one of the causes of depreciation. It is a decline in utility not directly related to physical usage or the passage of time.

Much of the perceived complexity of depreciation is related to the fact that an obsolescent property investment can increase in value, whereas the popular understanding of obsolescence is that it causes a decrease in value. Two factors explain this apparent problem.

Firstly, in a period of inflation property rents generally increase while yields might remain relatively stable (see Tables 5 and 6 in Chapter 3). As a result, obsolescence may be reflected not in falling values but in under-performance in relation either to inflation or to an index of prime property values. This explains the use of the word *real* in each of the above definitions. A loss in real value – depreciation – may therefore be explained as under-performance in relation to an index of newly prime properties.

Secondly, obsolete property can increase in *real* value as a result of advantageous planning decisions, such as permission for increasing the plot ratio of an office site. Obsolescence for the purposes of this research is quite independent of this factor, but confusion is created by the use by some writers (for example, Fraser, 1984) of the term *economic obsolescence* to explain under-utilisation of a site resulting from (for example) a valuable planning consent. This term is of no help in this analysis. According to this definition of economic obsolescence, a brand new, state-of-the-art low density development may be obsolete as it is built. To the investor who purchases the building secondhand this is not a factor which would be seen as a cause of depreciation. What is therefore of interest is obsolescence leading to depreciation in the *real existing use value* of a property investment.

Tenure-specific and property-specific depreciation

Depreciation in the real existing use value of a property investment may result from tenure-specific or property-specific factors. Tenure-specific factors are the results of leases, tenancies and statutes which restrict or encumber the investment. Property-specific depreciation, on the other hand, affects the property regardless of tenure.

Figure 1 shows these two sources of depreciation in real existing use value. The remainder of this chapter explains the expansion of the taxonomy.

An example of tenure-specific depreciation is the short leasehold, as its value falls purely as a result of the passage of time. (Note that this is not an obsolescence factor in the terms of the basic definition.) Down-rating of the quality of a tenant's covenant leading to increases in required yield is another example of depreciation which cannot be described as an obsolescence factor.

Tenure-specific depreciation is not of interest in this book. It is depreciation resulting from the property itself which forms the subject of this study. Assuming that subject properties are unencumbered freeholds with identical tenants and tenancies ensures that property-specific factors only will be considered.

Figure 1: A classification of depreciation and obsolescence

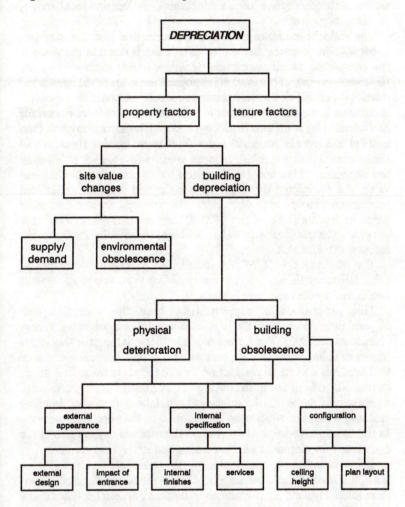

Site and value changes and building depreciation

The existing use value of a property investment may be notionally split into two parts: site and building. While the site value may increase or decrease in real terms over time as the result of a complex series of factors, the building value *must* decrease or depreciate in real terms.

Site depreciation is a misleading term because of this distinction. Site value changes may be caused by general demand/supply factors. These include the general level of economic activity; the general level of activity in the property market; the level of activity in the particular sector of the property market under consideration; and local activity in that sub-market.

The residual model of site value determination (see, for example, Darlow (1983)) states that the value of a site is equal to the value of the completed development less demolition and construction costs (including profit). If the market is buoyant, the value of the completed development will rise as rental values rise. If, as would be expected, there is no immediate and direct link between market forces of supply and demand for completed buildings and their construction costs, then costs would remain constant in the short term, causing the whole of the increase in value resulting from an upturn in the market to fall upon the site value. This may be illustrated by an example. The current value of a completed development is estimated to be £1,000,000 but increases over a period to £2,000,000. The development cost (including demolition costs and profit) is £400,000 and remains constant over the period. The residual site value is therefore initially £600,000 but increases to £1,600,000.

The whole of the £1,000,000 increase in completed development value falls upon the site; the notional building value therefore remains unaffected by demand/supply changes.

This proposition is supported by both the Ricardian/post-Keynesian/Marxian and the neo-classical schools of value theory (Lichtenstein, 1983). The former *objective* theory is based on the labour theory of value, which asserts that value is production-driven. Given that land has no cost of production and no labour is embodied within it, rewards to land are in the nature of a surplus. The rental value of a property is made up of a de-capitalised, labour-embodied building cost and a surplus, which may be assigned to the pure land element. In the example above, it is short-term fluctuations in the price of the completed development which are assigned to the land element.

Using the latter, neo-classical, *subjective* theory of value, rental value is a function of demand and supply. Against the background of a short-term relatively fixed supply, and given that the demand for office space is a derived demand, the rental value of office space in the City of London in the short term will depend largely on the demand for financial services. If the demand for financial services increases, occupational demand may rise relative to supply, and rent will increase. The cyclical nature of ocupational property markets results in fluctuating site values as rent increases and reduces in response to changes in the level of occupational demand. In contrast, the building depreciates; similar new buildings constructed upon identical quality sites are observed to attain higher rents.

Figure 2 illustrates this notional split by assuming straight-line building depreciation and constant site value over time and showing the point at which redevelopment is viable.

Figure 2: Redevelopment viability analysis

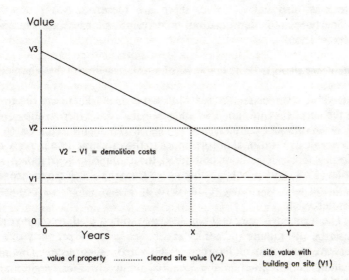

Simplistically, the point at which redevelopment becomes viable is when the site value exceeds the value of the existing property (building and site). However, it is necessary to distinguish between cleared site value and the value of the site with an obsolescent building upon it. Cleared site value is equal to the value of the site with obsolescent building *less* the cost necessary to clear the site. Redevelopment is therefore not viable at point X : existing use value (= V2) exceeds development value (= V2–V1), and the building cannot be said to be worthless or obsolete. At point Y, however, development value (= V1) and existing use value (= V1) equate, so that this is the point of redevelopment viability, and at this point the building is obsolete.

The total value of a property comprises depreciated building value (initially V3–V1, falling to V1 at the point of redevelopment), plus cleared site value (V2), less demolition costs (V2–V1). Thus, where TV = total property value, DBV = depreciated building value, CSV = cleared site value and DC = demolition costs,

$$TV = DBV + CSV - DC$$

Thus: $DBV = TV - CSV + DC$
At the point of redevelopment: $DBV = 0$
So that: $TV = CSV - DC$

In words, at the point of redevelopment the total property value is equal to the cleared site value less demolition costs. Given that the site may also fall in value, there are therefore two sources of property-related depreciation: site value changes and building depreciation.

Site value changes

Site value changes are the result of two factors. These are the result of the surplus/supply and demand relationship referred to above, and of *environmental obsolescence*. This is the factor referred to as economic or locational obsolescence in the previous discussion of the North American tradition embodied, for example, in Wurtzebach and Miles (1984) and must be distinguished from the obsolescence created by favourable re-zoning referred to by Fraser (1984) as economic obsolescence.

The term environmental obsolescence will be used from here on to describe the diminished utility and hence value of property due to negative environmental forces in the surrounding area. This may include changing use in the location, or unattractive neighbouring buildings. The result is a depreciation in site value. (A parallel is provided by the term worsenment (Davies, 1985).)

Building depreciation

Building depreciation is also the result of two distinct factors. *Physical deterioration* may be defined (following Wofford, 1983) as deterioration of the physical fabric of the building as a function of use and the passage of time, while *obsolescence* is differentiated (by Baxter, 1981) as a value decline not directly related to use or the passage of time. These are the broad definitions employed by Salway (1986) in the CALUS report. These distinguishing definitions are not yet acceptable, however. The action of the elements is an important consideration in the physical deterioration of buildings not referred to by Salway. Additionally, it is difficult to see how the passage of time creates deterioration other than as a result of use or the action of the elements. Hence physical deterioration is better defined as deterioration of the physical fabric of the building as a function of use and the action of the elements.

(Several writers, for example Baxter, 1981, refer to the *physical life* of a building as if it were a measurable function of physical deterioration. This concept should be rejected. Unless the structure actually collapses, physical life becomes testable only in economic terms, as it is dependent upon the relationship of maintenance costs, rental values and other factors. This is supported by Wurtzebach and Miles (1984).)

Obsolescence, in contrast to physical deterioration, is a value decline not directly related to use, the action of the elements or the passage of time. Obsolescence may be instantaneous as a result of a technological advance. It results from change which is extraneous to the building in question, such as changing market perceptions about such factors as quality and design.

Figure 1 shows the divisions between supply/demand factors and environmental obsolescence, and between physical deterioration and obsolescence as causes of site value change and building depreciation respectively. (It is not suggested that the preferred distinctions between site value change and building depreciation and between site and building value are perfect, and problems may arise in assigning both value and causes of depreciation to one to the exclusion of the other. For example, the effect of changing car parking requirements on the value of a property may be more accurately assigned to the *relationship* of the building and its site rather that to either factor in isolation.)

2. Forms of building obsolescence

Introduction

Typical US analyses of depreciation split building-related depreciation factors into two categories: physical deterioration and functional obsolescence. For the purposes of this research, as stated above, it is agreed that physical deterioration is too narrow a concept to cover all causes of building depreciation. Building obsolescence (including functional obsolescence) appears to be more important, and requires more exploration.

Categories of building obsolescence

Salway (1986) refers to further categorisations of building obsolescence. These are as follows:

i   aesthetic (or visual) obsolescence, resulting from outdated appearance;

ii functional obsolescence, the product of techological progress which causes changes in occupiers' requirements, impinging upon both layout and facilities offered;

iii legal obsolescence, resulting from the introduction of new standards (for example, safety regulations); and

iv social obsolescence, resulting from increasing demands by occupiers for a controlled environment and improved facilities.

Legal and social obsolescence can be regarded as sub-sets of functional obsolescence, which is thereby to be distinguished from aesthetic obsolescence. It is therefore possible to identify two major obsolescence types: these are *functional obsolescence* and *aesthetic obsolescence*.

It is now necessary to progress towards a model which can be used for the measurement of these two types of obsolescence. By breaking down the qualities of a building and their susceptibility to obsolescence, it is possible to move beyond a conceptual, and towards a practicable, model for its examination.

It is proposed to examine, first, how these two major obsolescence types act upon a building and second, the extent to which the major *qualities* of a building are subject to obsolescence.

3. Building qualities

The following distinction between three fundamental determinants of building quality is suggested as a useful basis for analysis by commentators on building design and depreciation reviewed in Section 2 of Chapter 3.

1. The *external appearance*, entrance hall and common parts of the building together produce a psychological and visual impact which may alter as market perceptions of design quality change, acting through aesthetic obsolescence to create building obsolescence.

2. The *internal specification*, affecting both the quality and quantity of finishes and services, will have both an aesthetic and functional impact as market demands change. The appearance of the interior may become inferior as fashions change, while the productivity of those who work in the building may be inhibited by outdated services and fittings. Both aesthetic and functional obsolescence result.

3. As technology progresses, buildings need to be sufficiently flexible to cope with raised floors, suspended ceilings, revised internal layouts and so on. A lack of flexibility is a source of functional obsolescence as the demands of a market change. *Configuration* is the horizontal and vertical layout of a building, which acts largely through functional obsolescence to make a building less useful (obsolescent) as requirements change.

Of the three building qualities noted above (external appearance, internal specification and configuration) certain qualities may be susceptible to both obsolescence and physical deterioration, so that a classification of the causes of obsolescence is less than straightforward. The external appearance of a building, for example, will be affected by obsolescence as fashions change, but also by deterioration, so that depreciation resulting from external appearance is a function of both factors. Similarly, internal specification and services will be subject to both obsolescence and deterioration. Of the three sources of obsolescence, only configuration is unaffected by physical deterioration. Depreciation is the combined result of obsolescence and deterioration.

4. A full taxonomy

A study of the literature relating to the building design aspect of depreciation (see Chapter 3, Section 2) shows that each of the basic building qualities (external appearance, internal specification and configuration) naturally breaks into further sub-factors and that a further distinction based on these subdivisions may be useful.

Firstly, external appearance is a function not only of the pure external design but also of the entrance hall to the building, which is clearly preceived as part of the *external* image. Individuals feel external to the building until admitted past the reception desk (see Healey and Baker, 1987).

Secondly, internal specification affects both the design and quality of internal finishes (doors, walls and so on) and the design and quality of services (lifts, air-conditioning, and others) (see Ferguson, 1987).

Thirdly, configuration is a function of both horizontal and vertical layouts, in other words of plan layout and of floor-to-ceiling heights (see Worthington, reported in Chapter 3, Section 2, and Pepper and Morgan, 1986).

Figure 1 shows the developed complex relationship of deterioration and obsolescence and of external appearance, internal specification and configuration, and the breakdown of the latter three factors into twin factors (external design and impact of entrance/common parts, internal finishes and services, and floor-to-ceiling heights and floor layout). These could be further classified into sub-factors for a more detailed analysis.

It has to be accepted that the classification shown in this model is neither finite nor beyond debate. For example, functional obsolesence may be difficult to divorce from aesthetic obsolescence as worker productivity will depend upon the design of a building as well as its environmental quality. Configuration, while shown as an input into functional obsolescence, might for similar reasons be a minor determinant of aesthetic obsolescence. In addition, environmental obsolescence is not easily divorced from supply/demand factors when the latter are defined to include local activity in a sub-market. Such local activity may, of course, be affected by the quality of local buildings, which is a cause of environmental obsolescence.

In conclusion, this is a highly complex area. Nonetheless, the classification developed in this chapter facilitates a meaningful examination of the relative importance of the broad sources of property investment depreciation. In summary, obsolescence is a *cause*; deterioration is a *cause*; depreciation is the *effect*.

Chapter 5

Methodology and data

1. Introduction

The CALUS study, Depreciation of Commercial Property (Salway, 1986), was the first major study in the UK of its type. It attracted considerable publicity and laid the ground for several more specific research projects, being a wide-ranging discussion of the problem of depreciation as seen from several standpoints. The report is largely descriptive, and derives from existing published material, but much original data are presented. It is therefore the major foundation for further research, and in addition provides the first serious empirical study in the UK.

Three areas of empirical research completed as part of the CALUS project are referred to in the summary section of that report. These are as follows.

1. A survey of users' views on the problems of older office and industrial buildings was carried out by means of a questionnaire survey of property managers of major listed companies. Forty-three questionnaires were completed. The findings are in relation to the identification and ranking of critical problems of older buildings, although no attempt was made to measure the impact of these problems upon rental value.
2. A survey of property investors' views and policies on depreciation was undertaken to obtain from investors their views of the likely life cycles of different building types and the related risk of their becoming unlettable.

    3. A cross-section survey of differences in value between new and
       older office and industrial buildings at June 1985 was carried out.

Data was derived from estate agents' opinions of the rental value and
investment (initial) yield of hypothetical buildings at 32 office and 25
industrial locations. The hypothesis used in this test was that the
(independent variable) building age determined the (dependent
variable) building value. This was intended to provide an insight into
the relationship of building depreciation and property values.

    Generalised conclusions are drawn from these studies. For example,
it is stated that on average the rental value of office buildings falls from
the index datum of 100 at age 0 years to 85 at age 5, 72 at age 10 and
55 at age 20 years respectively. From these figures it is concluded that
average depreciation rates are 3.3% over years 0 to 5, 3.4% over years
5 to 10 and 2.7% over years 10 to 20.

    Within these general conclusions it is of course true that major
variations are disguised. Not all buildings depreciate at the same rate:
if they did, while there may be wider implications across the capital
markets, the implications for investment choice within the property
market are minor. The degree to which this information is useful is
therefore restricted. In addition, the use of hypothetical data limits
the applicability of research findings. It is therefore necessary to
advance beyond the CALUS report to a more specific study of the
causes and effects of building depreciation, preferably based on a
sample of actual buildings, which will enable analysts to anticipate the
differential impact of depreciation on buildings of certain types.

2. Beyond CALUS: measuring the forces behind depreciation

Salway suggests that the next advances necessary in this type of research
are:

   i to expose the forces behind depreciation; and
  ii to set up analytical models which enable decision-makers to make
      due allowance for it.

Exposing the forces behind depreciation is a task begun in Chapter 4.
This establishes a classification model as the basis for further analysis.
In Chapters 6 and 7 an attempt is made to continue this task and gauge
the relative importance, and measure the relative impact, of these
forces. In Chapter 8 a depreciation-sensitive decision model for
property investment is developed. This work directly addresses the
Salway proposals, and attempts to advance research beyond the
CALUS report in the two directions specified.

Data analysis has been performed at each of two levels. Firstly, in order to produce an empirical comparison for the results of the CALUS study, depreciation is related to building age as a precursor to the main analysis. Secondly, in order to expose more meaningfully the forces behind depreciation, an attempt is made to identify and measure the impact of the causes of obsolescence and depreciation. This is the main research effort, predicated on the basis that age is a proxy for more fundamental causal variables, and suggesting the central hypothesis of this research: a model which incorporates the causes of depreciation provides a superior explanation of depreciation to one which relates depreciation to age alone.

Two data samples are used. Following Bowie (1982) and Salway, offices (Chapter 6) and industrials (Chapter 7) form the basis of the empirical work in this research. Chapter 3 provides justification for this choice.

Obsolescence can only be measured as a factor within depreciation. What is needed is therefore a measure of *building depreciation* within which obsolescence can be identified (see Chapter 4). This should initially be achieved by distinguishing site and building factors. Site value changes and building depreciation should be isolated in order to measure the latter; this is a first step towards an understanding of building obsolescence. Building depreciation, defined as a loss in the notional real existing use value of the building and not the site on which it stands, may be isolated by stripping out site factors from property-specific depreciation.

A measure of building depreciation should recognise the following.

1. The notional value of a building is almost impossible to measure. There is no means of identifying it other than as a residual after site value is removed from total property value (see Chapter 4). Given that evidence of site values is rare and likely to be highly imperfect, this presents enormous problems. The solution adopted in this research is to use property value as a proxy for building value, and to remove the effect of site changes by holding site value constant. This is achieved in two ways: firstly, by structuring a sample of properties within a tightly defined geographical area (125 office buildings within the central City of London area and 125 industrial buildings within a single estate) within which variations in site value are likely to be small; and, secondly, by smoothing property values in accordance with the small variations in location value that remain.

2. A loss in value is revealed as a shortfall in rental value and/or as an excess of all-risks yield against prime or best rents or yields. It may in addition be disguised by expenditure upon a building. The major research method chosen (see below) dictated

abstracting away from the need for and effect of expenditure. Hence the emphasis of the research method is in two parts: (i) a study of falling rental values; and (ii) a study of rising yields. These are addressed separately in the first instance, and only later are they combined in a study of capital value depreciation.

3. A loss in real property value is measured by comparing the value of each building in a data sample against an average prime or best value of similar property. Existing use value is isolated by compiling a data sample free of changes in use, and changing plot ratios are excluded by measuring property value on a unit of developed space basis.

3. Measurement methods

A loss in real property value is determined by occupiers and investors and evidenced in falling real rents and rising yields, which together create falling capital value. In order to measure building depreciation as a factor in property performance, therefore, it is necessary to examine both rents and yields. Performance may then be related simply to age, as in the CALUS report, or to building quality. Both relationships are explored in Chapters 6 and 7.

Building quality is based upon the classification developed in Chapter 4. In order to put this classification into effect, it is necessary to relate relative performance to physical deterioration and obsolescence factors (external appearance, internal specification and configuration).

Two alternative measurement methods may be adopted. These are:

i a longitudinal analysis; and
ii a cross-section analysis.

Longitudinal analysis

A longitudinal analysis, holding site factors constant, would track the performance of a sample of buildings over time. Losses in real existing use value for each building could then be related to age and to building qualities. There are, however, several difficulties with this approach. These may be listed as follows.

1. It is not possible to hold site factors constant over time. Certain sections of a location will improve while others decline due to environmental obsolescence and to shifts in supply and demand relationships. This will cloud the measurement of building

depreciation. It may not be an enormous problem in certain markets, given appropriately chosen boundaries, but it will inevitably be a source of noise or distortion.

2. It is difficult to find a sufficiently large data sample with full evidence of performance, which has to include rental values, yields and expenditures, over a sufficiently long period for a meaningful analysis.

3. Estimates of the quality of subject buildings in terms of external appearance, internal specification, configuration and physical deterioration factors can only be retrospective. It is therefore crucial that no changes have occurred over the measurement period, but this is unlikely, particularly given that obsolescence factors are extraneous to the subject property.

4. The cyclical nature of the market is another factor which may distort a measurement of building depreciation (Brown (1986), for example, suggests this problem). There is a suspicion that in times of high demand in the economy, and therefore high occupation demand, inferior buildings will let for as much as brand-new *state of the art* buildings, given a situation of low supply. The latter factor is perhaps explained by vigorous competition to occupy property, resulting in demand spreading to a wider range of properties. Such general economic conditions appear to act to reduce depreciation by forcing together the relative values of good and bad buildings. If this is the case, it appears curious that the rent differential is not maintained by the price of all accommodation increasing. Possible explanations for this are as follows.

(a) A rent barrier prevents the very best buildings from attaining relatively higher rents. This may be a result of a ratchet effect in the property occupation market, reinforced by the action of agents in that market.

Most measures of property rental values relate to *prime* rental values, that is the best rent(s) achieved in a given sub-market. In a particular location, the relationship of these prime rental values over a period show steep rises and plateaus (see, for example, Jones Lang Wootton, 1988). A contributory reason for this is the role played by letting agents, whose asking prices are based on rental valuations which are influenced by previous lettings. Only when very high levels of demand express themselves in great pressure on rental levels are these plateaus broken through. When they are broken through, rises can be very steep. The behaviour of prime rental values can disguise the movement in non-prime rents, which may be gathering behind the prime value to exert the very pressure which causes the change.

(b) A lack of supply of superior property (which would probably be the first to be let at the beginning of a period of high demand) means that there is no evidence in the market of deals at higher rents and lower yields, and also that there is no opportunity for demand to produce higher rents and lower yields other than for inferior buildings.

If an undersupplied market witnesses inferior properties letting/selling for amounts similar to high quality buildings, then the measurement of building depreciation and obsolescence in a cyclical market is made very difficult, as these phenomena would only become apparent in times of falling demand. The period chosen for a longitudinal study is therefore very important, and a neutral period may be impossible to identify over anything but a very long period.

For these reasons a longitudinal analysis may present considerable difficulties, which suggests that the alternative cross-section analysis should be considered.

Cross-section analysis

A cross-section analysis for the measurement of depreciation was favoured in the CALUS report. Salway measured depreciation by employing the age of buildings as a proxy for all factors contributing to building depreciation, and comparing the estimated rental values of hypothetical properties at one point in time in order to keep site and tenure factors constant. This analysis provided no information about obsolescence, as no attempt was made to examine the role of age as an indicator of obsolescence. However, that is not to say that it is impossible to measure obsolescence using Salway's type of approach. Given a data sample of findings in a given location, it is possible to measure the impact of building depreciation upon value relative to a market prime standard by comparing relative values of different buildings and to identify the effect of obsolescence within that impact. For example, buildings identical in all aspects except for layout will differ in value: the difference is accounted for by differences in layout, and conclusions regarding the impact of layout (an obsolescence factor) upon depreciation may thereby be made.

Nevertheless, there are also difficulties with a cross-sectional measurement method.

1. As values of the same building are not compared over time, and because buildings (especially offices) are largely heterogeneous, the method is less convincing as a controlled test of the depreciation of buildings. While it may be said in defence that

obsolescence is *not directly related to. . . the passing of time* (see Appendix A), differences between the buildings included in the sample inevitably reduce the validity of the test.

2. The impact of site factors cannot be perfectly isolated when buildings on different sites are compared. A longitudinal study does not suffer from this problem as long as relative site factors remain constant over time.

3. In a cross-section study there is a risk that any market imbalance or peculiarity distorts more *normal* patterns of depreciation (Salway, 1986). However, this may also be a problem with a longitudinal study: see above.

4. A cross-section study will not reveal the sudden onset of obsolescence by, for example, technological change (Salway, 1986).

5. It is impossible to examine the effect of expenditure as an indicator of depreciation within a cross-section study.

The preferred methods of analysis

It is suggested that both cross-section and longitudinal methods have a place in the estimation of depreciation and obsolescence and should ideally be used in tandem. Data constraints may, however, prevent the attainment of this ideal. It is stated above that depreciation may be realised in the rental value or the all-risks/initial yield of a building, and that it may be disguised by expenditure. The latter problem does not arise in the cross-section analysis; in a longitudinal analysis it has to be countered by rigorous checking of files relating to individual properties over the study period. A cross-section analysis is thereby easier to use. It is also true that data availability falls as the analysis period changes from a single cross-section point to a longitudinal time series, and as the number of observations within that series increases. Finally, the availability of information regarding yields over time is greatly limited by the way property information is typically kept, with greater emphasis being placed upon rental values. The limitations of a longitudinal analysis referred to above are therefore particularly relevant to yields.

In conclusion, use of a cross-section analysis is supported by the extra quantity and quality of the data that may be obtained, and this consideration is of over-riding importance in this research. A longitudinal study of rents is likely to be of use as a check. These considerations led to a two-part study of rental values, firstly by cross-section and secondly by means of a longitudinal study. This applies to both data samples, described below.

The data samples

Following Bowie (1982) and Salway (1986) the two data sets relate to office and industrial buildings. The major study (described in Chapter 6) is of City of London offices. A minor supporting study (described in Chapter 7) is of a very large industrial estate situated to the west of London.

4. Data preparation: offices

Selection of the data base

Cross-section studies are to be used as the major research method in the identification of the contribution of building obsolescence (and its causes) to depreciation. This necessitates the comparative examination of values of buildings of different ages and types at one point in time.

Differences in site value are likely to complicate such a comparative examination to an unacceptable degree. As sites in different locations rise and fall in value over time, differences in site value may also reduce the accuracy of a longitudinal test of building depreciation, also used in this research, albeit with a restricted sample. It is therefore highly advantageous in constructing a data sample of actual properties to exclude the effect of site value variations both between properties of similar size and type and within the value of a particular property over time. The requirements of a statistically significant data set are a constraint upon this, with the result that very few opportunities exist within the UK to collect an acceptable quantity of data within a sufficiently homogeneous (in terms of site values) location, particularly bearing in mind current requirements of confidentiality of data within the UK property market.

The requirements of the sample are two-fold: firstly, to minimise differences in locational value while, secondly, maintaining as large a potential data set as possible. The central part of the City of London, that is the area within a maximum radius of around one-third of a mile from the Bank of England, presents an opportunity to achieve this. The area broadly corresponds with the Central Banking Area and the southern/eastern sectors of the Outer Banking Area as defined in Richard Ellis' *City Property Forecast* (Richard Ellis, 1986).

The database comprises 125 office buildings, largely selected on the basis of familiarity to surveyors in the City office of Richard Ellis and/or inclusion in the *RICS/Actuaries Rent Index* (RICS/Institute of Actuaries, quarterly). The properties include examples of both refurbishments and original (that is non-refurbished) buildings, air-conditioned and non air-conditioned offices and a wide range of ages and styles.

In order to ensure that a useful and (to a limited extent) representative sample of City offices was the result of this method of data assembly, initial analyses of the data were carried out to identify inconsistencies and the study area was, as a result, redefined from the original. Inconsistencies were defined as very high or very low rental values per square foot in comparison to measured averages in the sample. Surveyors were questioned about outliers of this type. If there were good reasons for such inconsistencies, the data were dropped. This happened in the case of a small number of low rental value buildings, all of which were currently the subject of renovation or refurbishment and whose current rental values were therefore artificially low. Further more formal tests were carried out, and are described below.

It was also necessary to control the effect of varying locations within the study area, in order:

i   to ensure that wide variations in locational value did not exist; and
ii to smooth away any remaining minor variations.

The effect of location and its control is discussed in full later in this section (Location).

Testing the data sample

The major research effort related to the collection of rental data. For every property in the database, a panel of three surveyors familiar with the study area was asked to produce a consensus view of the current rental value (at August 1986) per square foot per annum on the assumption that a good quality tenant would be taking a typical new lease of a 10,000 sq ft unit within the building, as far as this was possible or appropriate. This achieved several purposes: among them, the fact that the rental opinion was based on a typical (25 years with 5-year reviews, full repairing and insuring) new lease excluded any distorting effects that might arise because of the unique circumstances and qualities of an actual tenant or lease contract. Also, the presumption of a 10,000 sq ft unit, coinciding as it did with the requirements of the RICS/Actuaries Office Rents Index, negates the effect of property size as a determinant of rental value. Differences in rental value can then be ascribed to physical qualities.

Those physical qualities likely to be most important were determined from a full list of possibilities by a brainstorming exercise in which four briefed agents arrived at a consensus view. Those identified qualities were used in developing the classification of depreciation and obsolescence presented in Chapter 4. The final choice, constrained to a list of five, was configuration of space, external appearance, internal specification and physical deterioration, plus siting. (The eventual exclusion of siting as a factor in the analysis is dealt with at a later stage: see *Smoothing the data sample* below.)

The three surveyors who made up the panel included two letting agents and a rent review specialist. The involvement of the latter acted as a moderating influence in the assessment of both rental value and building qualities (see below). Rental values were estimated by the panel in a single interview meeting. The panel were shown photographs of the 125 buildings and were given details of age, if and when refurbished, whether air-conditioned, and full addresses. Every building was familiar to at least one member of the panel.

The panel was asked to estimate the rental value which would be currently attainable in the market given a reasonable marketing delay and subject to all the qualifications noted above. All panel members had prepared valuations in advance of the discussion. Where valuations differed (and this was not uncommon, although the degree of variation was usually within 5%) a consensus view was arrived at by discussion in every case.

These data are not a measure of the market price of City office space, and to that extent it is flawed. However, actual letting values could not be of use as the basis of research such as this for two reasons. Firstly, the number of lettings in such a tightly defined area in a reasonably closely defined time period is extremely small. A reasonable but unscientific estimate made at the time of the research was that no more than 5 per cent of the sample had been the subject of an open market letting in that year. Secondly, most open market lettings are coloured in some way: by existing relationships between the landlord and tenant, by the payment of premiums, by variations in repairing terms, and by variations in other lease terms.

Consequently opinions of value are the only useful data type collectable in sufficient quality and quantity, and the opinions of letting agents and a rent review specialist in open discussion are used as a proxy for the open market negotiation process. Given that agents interfere in the pricing mechanism (see above), this is perhaps not as great a divergence from the open market as it might appear.

Additionally, if there is any bias in these opinions, this is not of importance as long as the bias is consistent. A bias is possible because letting agents would be expected to be optimistic; but inconsistency is unlikely, given that knowledge of the probable behaviour of tenants and potential tenants is very highly developed among letting agents. Consequently, while the opinions of letting agents cannot be guaranteed as a perfect proxy for the opinions and behaviour of tenants (and potential tenants), the fit would be expected to be very good.

Consistency

In order to check the consistency of the sample (in other words, to identify data which is defective and/or unrepresentative), age was initially related to rental value. The expectation (following Salway, 1986) was of a noticeable negative correlation. However, too high a correlation coefficient (say above 0.8) might invalidate the hypothesis of this research, namely that building quality is a more meaningful predictor or determinant of rental value than simple age (see Section 2 above). Too low a correlation coefficient (say below 0.4) on the other hand might suggest an unrepresentative or otherwise defective data sample, given the intuitively held belief (confirmed in the CALUS approach) that older buildings are worth less, *ceteris paribus*, than new ones.

However, it is clear that in relating building age to rental value there is a cut-off point in terms of age beyond which meaningless results will be obtained. For example, there may be no difference between the rental values of 1820 and 1890 buildings, but the difference in age is great. To cope with this problem a cut-off rate of 35 years was used, and any building constructed prior to 1950 is given a notional age of 35 years. (This reduces the degree to which the distribution is normal, a problem which limits the usefulness of certain statistical measures.)

Furthermore, where a property had been substantially refurbished, it would be incorrect to relate the age of the original construction to rental value. For example, a period property (notional age 35) which has been re-developed behind the existing facade would command a substantially higher rent than an original building of the same, or even a lower, age. Rental value was therefore related to building age or, where relevant, the period since a major refurbishment, whichever is the lower value.

Unequivocal definitions of a *major refurbishment* are, it has to be accepted, somewhat elusive. It cannot consequently be guaranteed that all data points are correctly allocated to categories of refurbishments or unrefurbished original buildings. It has also to be recognised that the refurbished period building is a different proposition to the refurbished 1950's or 1960's building. Recognition of this factor among other reasons prompted separation of the refurbishments sub-sample from the original buildings sub-sample and a further analysis of sub-sets within that sub-sample for the purpose of validating certain analyses and for much of the subsequent statistical work. In Chapter 8, some of the results of these further analyses are presented.

As an initial test of the data sample, therefore, analyses of the relationship between age and rental value were carried out for all buildings, for original buildings and for refurbishments.

However, a statistical test suggests that any differences in the results of the analyses of building quality against age may be the result of chance at the 95% level of confidence. A Chow test is designed to examine whether a given model applies to two different data sets (Chow, 1960). The test begins with the null hypothesis that the regressions are identical, and proceeds to see whether the null hypothesis may be rejected (see, for example, Pindyck and Rubinfeld, 1981). The model tested is a regression equation relating depreciation in rental value to four building qualities and the result is that the null hypothesis cannot be rejected (see Technical Appendix to Chapter 5). Consequently, it must be said that the same model is justifiably applied to both sets of data. This means that different results obtained in tests of depreciation in rental value against building quality may be the result of chance.

In Chapter 6, therefore, separate analyses of refurbishments and original buildings are not reported. Table 12 below and other analyses in this chapter deal with the whole sample.

Table 12: Relationship of rental value and age: all properties (offices)

Number of data points:	125
Mean age:	9.62 years
Standard deviation of age:	9.65 years
Mean estimated rental value (ERV):	£30.75 pa
Standard deviation of ERV:	£5.30 pa
Correlation coefficient (r):	− 0.588
Regression equation:	ERV = £36.20 − 0.322 age
Coefficient of determination of regression equation ($\overline{R} \wedge 2$):	34.4%
Significance (t)	8.83

Table 12 shows that age is a reasonable indicator of rental value. The variables of age and rental value are negatively correlated, as expected. A correlation coefficient of -0.588 is acceptable, and the coefficient of determination ($\overline{R} \wedge 2$) of 34.4% states that age is only a fair indicator of rental value while raising no serious doubts about the adequacy of the data sample. It was felt that this provided a promising foundation for the research.

Location

The effect of location had also to be tested in order to establish that the degree of variation in site values fell within an acceptably narrow range. In addition, it was not desirable to allow major variations in land values to remain within the database when the purpose of the exercise was to create a homogeneous (in terms of site values) sample. On the other hand, it would be impossible to construct a data base with no variation in site values (see Chapter 4).

To ensure that the site effect was kept to a minimum, the following test was carried out. As part of the main data-gathering exercise, each property in the sample was assigned a score of 1 to 5 by the valuation panel to represent low or high quality respectively in terms of the following definitions: "neighbours, siting and immediate environs, including accessibility, frontage, floor level (where appropriate), and adjoining uses, but excluding wider location factors". This recognised the fact that, even within a homogeneous site value area, specific location-related factors cannot be removed from the list of valuable features of a building. It also provided the opportunity to ensure that site value variations resulting from wider location considerations did not colour the sample.

A high quality building derived from the sample, with a site score of 5, was hypothetically *placed* at 21 of the different locations within the database and a rental value estimate made by the panel. The result was a minimum value of £35 per square foot per annum and a maximum value of £41 per square foot per annum, a variation of 14.6% on the higher value. The differences in rental value led to the exclusion of some low value outlying locations and their replacement by central properties. What remained was a range from £35.75 to £41 (slightly over 12%) and a high correlation ($r = 0.811$) between site score and rental value.

This test suggested two things: firstly, that the degree of variation was within reasonable limits; and secondly that wider location factors (for example, the possibility of the western part of the study area being preferred to the eastern part) were of little impact in influencing rental value. A coefficient of determination ($\overline{R} \wedge 2$) of 66% (see Table 13) suggests that two thirds of variations in site values are explained by the specific location factors listed above (neighbours, siting and immediate environs, and so on). The remaining one-third falls to be divided between wider location factors and sample error. It is therefore realistic to conclude that wider location factors, defined as differences in site value between different parts of the study area, unconstrained by existing developments and occupation, are not of major impact in the sample.

Table 13: Relationship of site score and ERV (offices)

Site score	ERV (£)
5	40.0, 41.0, 39.5, 40.25
4	38.0, 39.0, 38.5, 39.0, 38.5
3	38.0, 38.0, 36.5, 37.0, 38.5, 38.0, 39.5, 36.5, 37.75
2	36.5, 35.0

Regression equation: ERV = £33.79 + (£1.27 * site score)
Coefficient of determination of regression equation ($\overline{R}^2$) = 65.77%
Significance (t) = 6.71

A further test was carried out to check more precisely the effect of proximity to the Bank of England. Agents' opinions were to the effect that the area immediately adjacent to Bank is renowned as the most attractive location in the City. There is no doubt much truth in this, but it does not appear to be crucial to the accuracy of this research. Apart from the fact that few of the properties in the sample are close to Bank, results of a simple analysis suggest negligible differences in rental value. Dividing the sample into inner and outer zones actually produced a marginally higher average rent for the *outer* zone. The results therefore suggest no great location distortion caused by proximity to Bank in the sample.

Smoothing the data sample

Differences in site value complicate a comparative examination of values of buildings of different ages and types both at one point in time and over time. It is therefore necessary to exclude the effect of site variations from the sample of rental values. The choice of the central City office area reduced such variations to a minimum, given the constraint of a need for a statistically significant database; but site value variations remain within the sample as a result of differences in specific site factors (neighbours, immediate environs and so on).

Given that these factors account for two-thirds of all variation in site values and that all 125 locations were valued on a scale of 1 to 5 to measure the attractiveness of each location, the opportunity to smooth rental values to exclude that specific location factor is presented. From the 21 rent points taken (see Table 13) the average rental value for different site scores can be computed. As rounded, these are as shown in Table 14.

Table 14: Site scores and average ERV (offices)

Site score	Average ERV (£)
2	£35.75
3	£37.75
4	£38.50
5	£40.25

Note: no property was allocated a site score of 1

From these averages, weightings are computed as shown in Table 15.

Table 15: Site smoothing factors (offices)

Site score	Smoothing factor
2	£40.25/£35.75 = 1.1259
3	£40.25/£37.75 = 1.0662
4	£40.25/£38.50 = 1.0455
5	£40.25/£40.25 = 1.0000

These weightings were then applied to all 125 data points. The result is that two-thirds of value variations caused by site are smoothed away from the dataset, as all buildings are effectively assumed to occupy a high quality site.

The available data, therefore, are based upon the rental value of a sample of 125 central City office buildings, with most site value variations smoothed away and with major inconsistencies in the data sample tested for and (where necessary) removed. They have also to include appraisals of building qualities, which are described immediately below.

Appraisals

Rental value and age data

To summarise, the data available at this stage are as follows:

    i the estimated rental value per annum of 10,000 square feet of space in the subject property let on a new 25-year lease with 5-yearly reviews to a good quality tenant with no unusual lease-terms, as at August 1986;

   ii the siting score on a scale of 1 (poor) to 5 (excellent): no buildings attracted a site score of 1, so the effective range is 2 to 5;

  iii the smoothed rental value, based on (i) above and the site smoothing factor derived above; and

  iv the age of the sample properties or the period since a major refurbishment was carried out.

These data facilitated the initial testing of the sample for inconsistency and any apparent problems and allowed the smoothing away of variations in value resulting from different siting. They does not, of course, help in the major task of this research, as described at Section 2 above.

To restate that task, it is to expose the forces behind depreciation and to gauge the relative importance of those forces. Figure 2 in Chapter 4 shows the model used as a basis for explaining depreciation by classifying its causes, and this presents the basic model used to achieve the aim of the research.

Building qualities data

It is noted in Chapter 4 that depreciation may result either from tenure factors or property factors. Tenure factors are excluded from the data described to date by assuming unencumbered freehold tenure and by assuming consistent and standard lease terms and tenants. Of the remaining property factors, depreciation may be said to result from site or building. The differential effect of site factors has been removed to a considerable degree and as far as is reasonably possible, so that remaining differences in value can be assigned to differences in building quality. Within the cross-section study, given that the definition of building depreciation for the purpose of this research is a loss in the real existing use value of a property investment, then (in the rental value context) any shortfalls in value against a prime index can be attributed to building depreciation. The prime index is represented by a rent of £40.25, the average rent for a prime building with a site score of 5 (an excellent site); shortfalls are represented by the difference between this figure and the actual smoothed rental values of the 125 buildings in the sample.

The shortfall in each case is caused by building depreciation resulting from differences in building quality. In order to relate the shortfall to building quality it is necessary to measure the latter.

Two root qualities are identified in Figure 1: physical deterioration and building obsolescence. It may have been possible to grade each building in the sample in terms of these twin factors. However, while physical deterioration of both internal and external building components can easily be scored in this way, building obsolescence is a highly complex factor which would create enormous difficulties. At the very minimum, it was considered necessary to subdivide building obsolescence into three distinct factors, as shown in Figure 1, each independent of the additional effect on physical deterioration. The three obsolescence factors are therefore:

i   the external appearance of the building, combining external design and the impact of the entrance, and so on, but ignoring the effect of physical deterioration upon this;
ii the internal specification, combining internal finishes and services but excluding the effect of physical deterioration upon each; and
iii configuration, combining floor-to-ceiling heights and floor layout, upon which physical deterioration has no effect.

Building quality and hence building depreciation can therefore be measured by assessing each building in terms of four major factors:

i   physical deterioration of both interior and exterior;
ii external appearance (external design and impact of entrance, and so on) ignoring the effect of physical deterioration;
iii internal specification (internal finishes and services) ignoring the effect of physical deterioration; and
iv configuration (floor-to-ceiling height and floor layout).

The selection of these factors was firstly confirmed as acceptable by discussion with the panel of valuers. The *measurement* of these factors was achieved by repeating the method employed to check site quality. The panel of three valuers, each highly familiar with the study location, was asked to produce, during four 3-hour sessions, a consensus view of the quality of each of the 125 buildings in term of the above four factors. A scale of 1 to 5 was again used, with the following implications.

1. Poor (in terms of physical deterioration, this means highly deteriorated)
2. Mediocre
3. Average
4. Good
5. Excellent (in terms of physical deterioration, this means a brand new building or equivalent)

(It would of course be possible to go beyond this classification into greater detail by measuring the quality of sub-factors. As a result of the occupier survey described in Chapter 6, this was attempted in the case of configuration. The global configuration score used in the main analysis is found by summating the separate scores for floor to ceiling heights and floor layout and dividing by two.)

The results obtained from the first round of question/answer sessions include the following:

   i   the building code number;
   ii the building age;
  iii whether refurbished (R) or not (0);
   iv the ERV of the building at August 1986;
   v the site score;
   vi the smoothed ERV;
  vii the physical deterioration score;
 viii the internal specification score;
   ix the external appearance score; and
   x the configuration score.

With this data it was possible to proceed with the cross-section rent analysis described in Chapter 6. Further similar appraisals were carried out to test the relative impact of curable and incurable depreciation: these are also described in Chapter 6.

Table 16 below shows means and ranges (standard deviations) of the appraisals for all buildings. This shows very similar ranges of scores for all qualities with the highest means for siting and external appearance, in that order. The mean for configuration is clearly the lowest, which suggests that the sample buildings fall short of market expectations by the greatest amount in respect of this factor. This probably reflects the impact of the impending *Big Bang* upon the market, as described in Chapter 3.

Table 16: Analysis of appraisals (offices)

	Mean	Standard deviation
Configuration	2.78	0.80
Internal specification	3.04	0.98
External appearance	3.33	0.99
Siting	3.58	0.86
Deterioration	3.10	1.00

Yield data

A cross-section yield analysis requires the addition of further data. Firstly, yields for unencumbered freehold sales of the 125 buildings (defined as rental value divided by price assuming a sale in the market as at August 1986) have to be estimated. Secondly, it is necessary to consider whether any factors not considered in the first round of appraisals are likely to distort or affect yields, and if so to measure and possibly smooth away the impact of these factors.

A second round of brainstorming sessions was carried out with a second (different) group of three valuers, all experts in the City office investment market. It was apparent from discussions with this second valuation panel that a new factor, lot size (defined as the outlay needed to purchase the investment) was considered to be of great impact on the market price and yield. This was tested by assigning scores on a scale of 1 to 5 for lot size using building area as a proxy for the necessary outlay. The scores had the meanings shown in Table 17.

Table 17: Lot size scores (offices)

Score	Lot size (sq ft)		
5	0	-	10,000
4	10,000	-	20,000
3	20,000	-	50,000
2	50,000	-	100,000
1	> 100,000		

Given the views of the second valuation panel, a high correlation between yields and lot size was expected: and the correlation should be negative, as a high lot size score should produce a lower yield. This was tested by estimating the correlation coefficient between yield and lot size. Given the effect of site on rental value, the correlation between yield and site was compared with the correlation between yield and lot size to establish the relative importance of these factors. The results were:

Yield and lot size: $r = -0.593$
Yield and site score: $r = -0.189$

It is apparent from these results that lot size exercises a much greater influence on yield than site. However, it is possible that a high correlation between lot size and site score is distorting the relationship. If the smaller lots are on the poorer sites, so that lot size and site score are highly negatively correlated, then there may be a stronger relationship between site score and yield than a correlation coefficient of – 0.189 suggests. In fact the correlation between lot size and site score is negative, but not high (– 0.229). It therefore appears that lot size has a considerably greater influence on yield than does site.

It was decided in an attempt to achieve a more meaningful analysis of yield depreciation to smooth out the effect of lot size from yield, just as the effect of site value had been smoothed out from rental value. (For site score and estimated rental value, r = 0.636; for lot size and yield, r = – 0.593, so that the effect is of similar weight.) It was decided not to smooth out the effect of site score on yield. Firstly, the impact is too small; and secondly the smoothing of data inevitably reduces its realism, so that double smoothing for lot size and site score would be a considerable step away from the raw data collected. (In an analysis of capital values (see Chapter 6), both lot size and site effects are, however, smoothed away by combining smoothed yields and smoothed rental values.)

The results obtained from the second round of panel sessions were:

   i   the building code number;
  ii   the estimated market yield for the property at August 1986;
 iii   the lot size; and
 iv   the yield smoothed for the effect of lot size.

Smoothing factors were calculated on a slightly different basis to that used in the rental smoothing process. While it had been possible to assess the rental value of a single building on different sites and to calculate from those results the average rental of that building on sites of different value, this was not thought to be a practicable approach for yields and lot size. The same building could not be imagined in different lot sizes so such a process would be straying too far from reality. Instead, therefore, the average yield for each lot size was calculated and weightings were based on ratios derived from those average yields. This was achieved as shown in Table 18.

It is interesting that yield does increase significantly at higher lot sizes. There are major, and stepped, increases in yield for properties over 20,000 square feet (0.6%) and for properties over 100,000 square feet (0.4%). (This information is of particular interest in the light of proposals for a unitised property market: see Adams and Baum (1989).)

Further data

The appraisals for yields and rental values can be simply combined to produce cross-section data for notional capital values. An analysis of these data is described in Chapter 6. It represents the third and final cross-section study for the City office sample.

Table 18: Lot size smoothing factors (offices)

Size (sq ft)	Size score	No of properties	Average yield (%)	Smoothing factor
< 20,000	4 and 5*	40	5.24	5.24/5.24 = 1.0000
20,000 - 50,000	3	34	5.84	5.24/5.84 = 0.8973
50,000 - 100,000	2	25	6.08	5.24/6.48 = 0.8618
> 100,000	1	26	6.48	5.24/6.48 = 0.8086

Note: * for a size score of 5 (up to 10,000 sq ft), the average yield is 5.25%; for a size score of 4 (10,000 to 20,000 sq ft), the average yield is 5.23%. As there is no significant difference, these categories are combined, with an average yield of 5.24%.

5. Data preparation: industrials

Selection of the data base

The industrial database comprises 125 properties within a closely confined area, spread fairly evenly over a very large (7.2 million square feet and around 350 units) trading estate to the west of London. This particular estate was selected for its size and homogeneity, and because data was likely to be relatively rich and consistent given its undivided ownership by a publicly quoted property investment and development company which provided full access to relevant information.

The sample of 125 was selected from a total of around 750 with a generally common locational advantage. No part of the estate was considered markedly superior to any other part, although certain road frontage properties were excluded from the analysis as their inclusion would tend to bring wider location factors into play (which would be both distorting and would reduce comparability with the City office research). Around the rest of the estate location was not generally considered to be a relevant factor, although accessibility and immediate environs (micro-location) within the estate may affect rents.

The sample of 125 was structured to be representative of the population in terms of age, size, type of construction (there are several standard unit types), refurbishment and spatial distribution. Around 42% of the buildings in the sample are pre-war; the rest are spread relatively evenly between 1950's, 1960's and 1970's properties, with some 1980's additions. Nineteen buildings in the sample have been refurbished at some stage, and 18 of these refurbishments were to pre-war buildings. Unlike the City office sample, there was little evidence to suggest that meaningful results would be produced by splitting the sample into original buildings and refurbishments.

Testing the data sample

Rental values

The collection of data for the industrial sample was generally carried out following the model developed for the office data. For this reason, the report of data preparation for industrial property is kept brief. There are, however, some differences in method which should be noted. It was not necessary to access rental values by means of a brainstorming session due to the common ownership and the regular formal valuations by the owners (every three years on average). For the purposes of the cross-section analysis, therefore, rental values used were taken directly from a formal and reported 1986 valuation of the properties. Rental values in the longitudinal analysis are based on a series of valuations at 3- to 5-year intervals.

These valuations expressly take no account of unusual lease terms, tenants, and so on, and therefore there are no tenure factors influencing rental value. If the tenants have not fulfilled all their repair obligations, the rental valuation assumes that they have done so, which could lead to problems when comparing rental value and building quality, but it appears that in only a small number of cases would the above assumption significantly affect the rent.

The analysis of yields for this sample would have been unlikely to produce useful results given the particular assumptions underlying the valuations. It was therefore decided not to analyse yields or (as a consequence) capital values for the industrial sample. The analysis is restricted to a comparison of the cross-section analysis of 125 buildings with a longitudinal analysis based on a set of samples of between 68 and 104 properties.

Factors influencing rental values

Agents and estate managers concerned with the estate were asked to list the five factors they considered to be of most importance in affecting tenants' location decisions and rents paid. Five factors were finally agreed on, and details of these are listed below.

1. *Unit size*: this is the floorspace of the particular unit in square feet.

2. *Office content*: this is the percentage of the floorspace given over to offices.

3. *Building quality:* this refers primarily to the external appearance of the building and type of construction. An attractive building projects a good image for the occupying company, and will therefore be scored highly for building quality. The use of quality materials in the construction, type of structure and general modernity of the building will also affect the building quality score. Factors such as the quality of the interior, the internal layout and provision of services are not specifically taken into account, except in so far as they may be reflected in the appearance of the building. Building quality can therefore be taken as a global score for the physical characteristics of the building in question.

4. *Site cover, loading, car parking, and so on:* this factor can be summarised as describing the flexibility of the building within its site. The site cover is the ratio of building area to site area, which will tend to influence both loading and car parking. A high site cover will tend to make loading and turning of vehicles difficult. Furthermore there will be less room for car parking. Buildings with an easily accessible loading bay (preferably covered) will tend to be scored highly, as will buildings with a high number of car spaces in relation to the size of the building itself.

5. *Accessibility and immediate environs*: this refers to location within the estate, and given that no part of the estate is thought to be significantly better than any other part it is a measure of micro-location, taking into account such factors as adjoining users, quality of buildings in the immediate vicinity, the road on which the property is located and whether or not the building occupies a corner site. For example, a corner building on the major road through the estate would tend to score highly because it is prominent and easily accessible. On the other hand a building tucked away in a narrow street would be given a low score because it is difficult to find, it is inaccessible and it has a poor environment.

Every building in the sample was scored (on a 1 to 5 scale) for each of these factors. For building quality, site cover and accessibility the following scale applied:

1. Poor
2. Mediocre
3. Average
4. Good
5. Excellent

Unit size and office content were scored according to pre-defined size bands as shown in Tables 19 and 20.

Table 19: Unit size scores (industrials)

Score	Lot size (sq ft)		
5	0	-	3,499
4	3,500	-	7,999
3	8,000	-	14,999
2	15,000	-	24,999
1		>	25,000

Table 20: Office content scores (industrials)

Score	Office content (%)		
5		>	30.00
4	15	-	29.99
3	10	-	14.99
2	5	-	9.99
1	0	-	4.99

Consistency

As in the office work, the initial analysis carried out related the age of the property to its 1986 rental value. However, this was of reduced interest for the industrial data, due to the similarity in the (high) average age of the sample building and the resulting heavily skewed distribution.

To avoid particularly misleading results it was decided to use a cut-off age of 40 years. All buildings built before 1946 were therefore presumed to be 40 years old at 1986. Again, where a property had been substantially refurbished, it would have been incorrect to use the original age of the property in an analysis of age and depreciation, and suitable adjustments were therefore made.

Smoothing the data sample

All rental values and depreciation levels used in the cross-sectional analysis of the industrial sample were smoothed to remove the effect of lot size. Table 21 shows correlations between the five property factors and smoothed rental values at 1986.

Table 21: Correlations between building qualities and rental value (industrials)

Quality	Correlation coefficient
Size	0.611
Office content	0.131
Building quality	0.521
Site cover, etc	0.226
Accessibility	0.131

Size appears to play the most important role in affecting rental values. An initial multiple regression model testing the relationship of the five factors and rental value at 1986 showed that by far the most important variable was unit size. Its significance was twice the magnitude of the next most important factor, and its coefficient was also greater. In addition, a survey of occupiers on the estate revealed that the most important factor affecting location decisions and rental value is unit size. (These tests are described fully in Chapter 7.) It was therefore considered appropriate to remove the effect of size on ERV so as to allow the relative importance of the other factors on a common unit of space to become apparent. This was achieved by applying a smoothing factor to all rents so that the smoothed rent reflects what that property would be let for if it were to fall within size band 5. Table 22 shows average ERVs for given size bands within the sample.

Table 22: Unit size scores and average ERV (industrials)

Size band	Average ERV
1/2	3.89
3	4.17
4	4.46
5	5.57

Table 23 shows the computed smoothing factors derived from Table 22.

The data fields used in the industrial study are listed in Chapter 7, Sections 2 and 4. Because of the nature of the analysis in the longitudinal test, unsmoothed rental values have been used. It is suggested that these two data sets (and especially the office data) are both very large and highly consistent as measures of the value and quality of buildings. Good quality property data of this type are extremely difficult to assemble in quantity. Consequently, a valuable and rare opportunity to undertake detailed empirical analysis is presented. The office and industrial analyses are described in Chapters 6 and 7 respectively.

Table 23: Unit size smoothing factors (industrials)

Size band	Smoothing factor
1/2	£5.57/£3.89 = 1.432
3	£5.57/£4.17 = 1.336
4	£5.57/£4.46 = 1.249
5	£5.57/£5.57 = 1.000

Technical appendix to Chapter 5

The Chow test for the stability of equations

This appendix shows the calculation used in testing the hypothesis that there is no statistical difference between the equations estimated for original and refurbished buildings.

The test statistic is defined as:

$$F = \frac{(SSR_N - SSR_{N1} - SSR_{N2})/K}{(SSR_{N1} + SSR_{N2})/(N - 2K)}$$

which is distributed as an F-distribution with $(K, N - 2K)$ degrees of freedom.

The terms are:

SSR_N = sum of squared residuals resulting from running a regression containing all observations of original and refurbished buildings

SSR_{N1} = sum of squared residuals resulting from a regression consisting of original buildings only

SSR_{N2} = sum of squared residuals resulting from a regression consisting of refurbished buildings only

K = number of regression parameters (coefficients) estimated

N = number of observations

Substituting the appropriate values:

$$F = \frac{(819.63 - 291.78 - 484.66)/5}{(291.78 + 484.66)/(125 - 10)} = 1.28$$

This value is less than the value for $F(5,115)$ at the 5% significance level (2.30) and the null hypothesis of no difference between the two regression equations cannot therefore be rejected.

Chapter 6

An analysis of property investment depreciation and obsolescence 1: City offices

1. Introduction

Chapter 5 describes the collection and preparation of two sets of data, each set describing 125 properties. The first, and major, set concerns offices in the central area of the City of London.

This chapter describes the analysis of the major data set and the collection and analysis of further data as both a check upon, and as an expansion of, the main analysis. It falls into five parts:

i a cross-section analysis of rental values, relating depreciation in rental values firstly to age and secondly to a set of building quality variables, including a subsidiary test of the relative importance of curable and incurable depreciation (Section 2);

ii a longitudinal analysis of rental values, repeating the main analysis described in Section 2 (Section 3);

iii a description and analysis of an occupier survey, further checking some of the results described in Sections 2 and 3 (Section 4);

iv a cross-section analysis of yields, relating depreciation in yield firstly to age and secondly to the same set of building quality variables referred to at (i) above (Section 5); and

v a cross-section analysis of notional capital values derived directly from rental value and yield data, relating depreciation in capital value to the same set of building quality variables referred to at (i) above (Section 6).

Conclusions are drawn in Section 7.

Hypothesis

In the introduction to Chapter 1 of this book the twin objectives of the research, the necessary advances beyond the work described in the CALUS report, were identified, and in Section 2 of Chapter 5 they were further discussed. The first of these is: **to expose the forces behind depreciation.**

In Chapter 4 a taxonomy of depreciation is built. This enables those forces to be identified. It is now necessary to gauge the relative importance, and measure the relative impact, of those forces: obsolescence, deterioration, and sub-factors within those categories.

In the CALUS report, depreciation was related to age, in order that depreciation rates over time may be estimated. In such an analysis, age is acting as a proxy for declining building quality, which is itself a combination of sub-factors (see Chapter 4). Given that these building quality factors vary between buildings and between sub-sectors of the property market, relating depreciation to building qualities will be more useful than relating it to age. This produces the major hypothesis of this research, which is as follows: **a model which incorporates the causes of depreciation provides a superior explanation of depreciation to one which relates deprecation rate to age alone.**

Data

Chapter 5 describes the data collection and preparation process. The result of the process is two unusually large and consistent property data sets which provide the opportunity for a full empirical analysis. The City office data are particularly promising in this respect.

The methodology used in this particular (and in most other) empirical analysis is a combination of hierarchical and statistical approaches (see below). This is intended to combine the views of experts with the objective test afforded by regression analysis and other statistical methods. It has already been shown that a hierarchical approach has so far driven the process of data preparation: in Chapter 4, a classification model is developed from the views of commentators on building design and depreciation, while Chapter 5 describes how a panel of expert valuers confirmed the selection of building quality factors before proceeding to assign values to them.

A linear relationship?

The method of statistical analysis chosen will depend upon the nature of the relationships between dependent and independent variables. These may be linear; alternatively, any of many types of non-linear relationships may be represented.

There is some strength in an argument that, *a priori*, non-linear relationships may exist within this data. Estimated rental value (ERV) against age, for example, is arguably likely to be non-linear as rental value will reach a minimum value which will be unaffected by age beyond a certain limit.

Figure 3 is a scatter diagram which shows the relationship between age and ERV. It can perhaps be said to support the suggestion that a non-linear relationship exists: specifically, ERV may appear to decline at a decreasing rate as age increases. Alternatively, a straight line can be driven through the scatter with some confidence, especially over years 0 to 20. A straight line relationship over this period is confirmed by the findings of Salway (1986), who found straight line deprecation in ERV over years 0 to 20 in his national survey. It is also true to say that it is depreciation patterns over this period which are of most interest, as the impact of depreciation in an appraisal model (see Chapter 8) will be greatest in the early years.

Figure 3: Scatter diagram: ERV against age

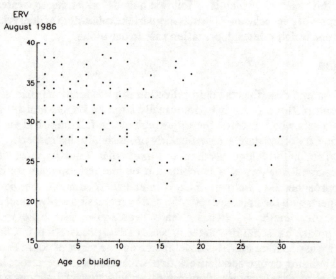

For yield against ERV, it is difficult to identify a relationship from visual examination of a scatter diagram, as Figure 4 shows. Perhaps an upward-sloping straight line relationship describes the best fit. It is similarly difficult to describe the relationship of ERV and building quality. Figure 5 shows the relationship of ERV and configuration score: arguably, this can again be represented by an upward-sloping straight line.

Figure 4: Scatter diagram: yield against age

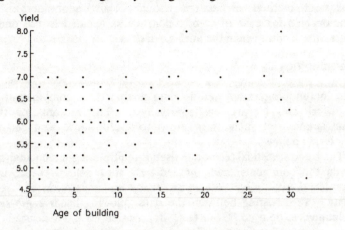

Figure 5: Scatter diagram: ERV against configuration

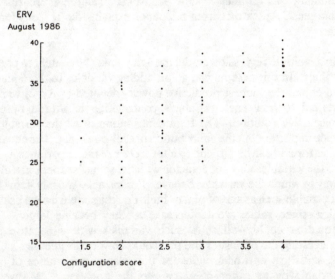

To conclude, there is both *a priori* and empirical evidence of a non-linear relationship between age and ERV. However, it is not clear. Additionally, over the first 20 years, the relationship may well be straight line. For other relationships, a straight line relationship describes the scatters as well as any other; *a priori*, there is little reason to suspect that a more complex pattern exists. Also, the instruction given to the panel of valuers was designed to establish a linear relationship between ERV and yield and the four building qualities. A change in score of one unit within but not between each category should be assumed to lead to the same change in rental value. Given the complexity of non-linear regression analysis, and given that a consistent method of analysis should ideally apply across all relationships for ease of comparison, it was decided to use linear regression techniques in the analysis of data.

Methodology

The methodology employed in data analysis is a combination of statistical and hierarchical approaches. The reasons for this amalgamation of techniques are introduced above and further developed below.

The basic statistical technique used is multiple regression analysis. Given the comments made immediately above, this is made less complex than it might otherwise be by an assumption of linear relationships existing between the data, allowing linear regression techniques to be used. Greaves (1984) considered and measured the determinants of residential property values using a similar approach, combining hierarchical and statistical (multiple regression) techniques. An extract from his paper explains the reasons for his choice:

> In a multiple regression model the analyst may be content to predict values. In this case he can go on adding variables to the equation to obtain the highest predictive power (denoted by $\bar{R}^2$) without regard to how each variable's contribution is altered by each successive addition. The total contribution of all the variables is then important but the contribution of each one is not. The equation thus formed can be difficult to interpret since the importance it gives to the variables may not coincide with the valuer's experience of the way in which the variables behave. For instance we may know that a variable such as size of plot or built-up area should have a positive sign, since values would increase as they became larger. The equation could well show such variables with a negative sign suggesting the opposite, and this could be very disquieting. . .
>
> A statistical approach indicates the relative importance of each variable by its order of entry into the equation. However, if multicollinearity is present to any extent in the sample, the statistical order of entry and hence the relative importance of each variable may not agree with that as seen by the hierarchical approach, which is based on the population. For this reason, if the analyst wishes to explain as well as predict values the selection of variables by a statistical approach may be inadequate. It should, therefore, be used as a check on the hierarchical approach if strong reasons exist to support the latter.

. . .a simple approach is necessary as a start and a logical starting point must be the market-place. The analyst should initially try to elicit from the consuming public, by a set of discerning and properly structured questions, the factors they are willing to pay for and in what order of priority they are placed.

Greaves distinguishes statistical approaches (the basis of the analysis described above) from hierarchical approaches by making the point that a multiple regression model may throw out a different ranking of variables from that which is consciously part of the decision process followed by consumers. If the research were to ignore a hierarchical approach, it is possible that the conclusions of the research in respect of the relative importance of building qualities may be incorrect.

Similar considerations drive the selection of methodology in this research, both Chapter 6 and Chapter 7. The prime motivation of the empirical research is the *explanation* of depreciation; a subsidiary aim is to enable a decision model to feed from the explanatory results by enabling a pragmatic prediction to be made. Neither aim is served by a purely statistical approach, nor by the construction of multiple regression models with a large number of independent variables which are needed to support high coefficients of determination.

Additionally, it is expected (and it is confirmed in this chapter) that multicollinearity will affect the multiple regression analysis. Where multiple regression analysis is used to explain the impact of several independent variables upon the dependent variables, and where there is some positive correlation between the independent variables, it is possible that the regression equation may be misleading as an indicator of the importance of the independent variables individually. For example, the importance of a variable may be much lower in the equation than is the case in reality, because the effect of changes in that variable upon changes in the dependent variable may be accounted for by another variable. Coefficients cannot therefore be relied upon as relative measures of the importance of individual variables. The sign of coefficients may even be reversed, so that the intuitive may not equate with the statistical effect of a particular variable.

The problem of potential divergence between hierarchical and statistical results becomes greater as the number of independent variables increases and with the degree of correlation between them. In this research, degrees of correlation are high: see, for example, Table 27. It is therefore helpful to impose a limit on the number of independent variables by using a hierarchical approach in their selection.

The usefulness of an explanatory model for forecasting is enhanced greatly by simplicity and by a control on the amount of data to be input. Again, therefore, the requirement within a decision model for a forecast of depreciation urges a limit on the number of independent variables in multiple regression equations.

These considerations have guided the methodology of Chapters 6 and 7. A hierarchical approach is first used to select variables. This has combined a search of published material (Chapter 3) and a panel consensus (Chapter 5). It is also checked by a survey of occupiers (Section 4, below). Regression models are then used to describe the relationship between age and ERV and between the four building qualities and ERV. The four-variable building quality equations may then be adjusted by removing variables, both to reduce problems of multicollinearity and to build a useful framework for prediction. The result is a series of relatively robust equations broadly consistent with a hierarchical ordering of importance, which can act as the basis for development of predictive models in Chapter 8.

2. Cross-section rent analysis

Age against depreciation in ERV

Table 24 shows the results of a comparison of age and smoothed depreciation in estimated rental value (ERV) at August 1986.

Table 24: Age against rental value

No of properties	125
Mean age	9.62
Mean smoothed ERV (£)	32.33
Mean depreciation (£)*	7.92
Standard deviation (age)	9.65
Standard deviation (ERV: £)	5.01
Regression equation:	
Depreciation (£) =	4.81 + 0.324 age
Coefficient of correlation (r)	− 0.623
Coefficient of determination (R^2) (%)	38.79
Significance (t)	8.83

Note: * against a prime rent of £40.25

The more depreciated is the building, the lower is its rent. Following Salway (1986) older buildings let for less. Hence depreciation in ERV and age are positively correlated, as Table 24 confirms. The results are highly significant at the 95% level showing that the first is not likely to be the result of chance; but only 38% of depreciation is explained by age, so other factors are clearly of importance.

In comparison to the initial test results described in Table 12 (Chapter 5) these results show that the effect of smoothing away site differentials has been to increase the correlation coefficient slightly, from 0.588 to 0.623. This suggests that the site factor was clouding the relationship to some extent, but the result still leaves room for a conclusion that age by itself does not provide a particularly good explanation of rental value and hence building depreciation.

Around 39% of the depreciation of all buildings is explained by the ageing process *per se*. Building qualities may provide a better explanation of depreciation: see below. The measure of explanation used is $\bar{R}^2$ (R bar squared), the adjusted coefficient of determination. R^2 is a measure of goodness of fit for a multiple regression equation and $\bar{R}^2$ is an adjusted value to take account of degrees of freedom which urges a reduction in the number of independent variables used (Thomas, 1983). This is of some value in this research: see Equation 10 and the preceding text (below).

Table 25 presents a clearer picture of the uneven pattern of rental depreciation connected with the ageing process. This shows high depreciation for years 17 to 26 (mean ages for each respective age band) for the whole sample. This is illustrated in Figure 6.

Table 25: Depreciation in ERV and age band (sample: 125)

Age	Frequency	Mean age	Average smoothed ERV (£)	Index	Dep'n pa (%)	Years
0-4	48	1.94	34.76	100		
5-9	31	6.77	33.12	95.28	0.977	2-7
10-14	19	11.26	32.16	92.52	0.615	7-11
15-19	10	16.70	31.22	89.82	0.496	11-17
20-29	8	26.13	25.37	72.99	1.785	17-26
30 +	9	34.44	24.40	70.20	0.336	26-43

Mean annual depreciation rate: 0.92%

Figure 6: Age bands and depreciation* in ERV

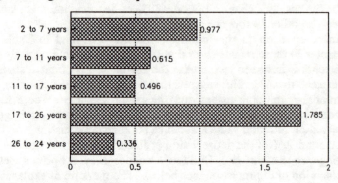

Note: * depreciation expressed as % per annum

Building qualities against depreciation in ERV

Age was found to be a useful, but imperfect, explanation of building depreciation. Building quality is now examined as a possible improvement upon this.

Depreciation is defined as the difference between the smoothed ERV of each property in the sample and the prime rent of £40.25. In order to test the relationship between building qualities and depreciation in ERV, the resulting depreciation figure in each case is compared with the shortfall in each of four building qualities against a prime score of 5, based on the hypothesis that a prime building scoring 5 in each of the four categories (physical deterioration, internal specification, external appearance and configuration) will let at a prime rent, once site effect is smoothed away. A positive relationship should therefore exist between depreciation and the shortfall in building quality score in each case.

The relationship is expressed in terms of the dependent variable (depreciation, that is £40.25 minus the smoothed ERV) and the independent variable (shortfall in the relevant building quality, that is 5 minus the relevant score), and is measured initially by means of the individual correlation coefficient.

Results are shown in Table 26.

The correlations are all high. Note that the correlation coefficient relating the independent variable (age) and the dependent variable (depreciation) was 0.623; it is therefore to be concluded that any one of the building qualities noted above is a stronger determinant of depreciation than age.

Table 26: Depreciation and building qualities (sample: 125)

Independent variable	Correlation coefficient
Internal specification	0.794
Physical deterioration	0.741
Configuration	0.702
External appearance	0.693

However, it is tempting but dangerous to conclude from these results which is the most important building quality. It appears that shortfall in internal specification is the best predictor of deterioration and hence the most important factor. While this is later shown to be the case it cannot be said at this stage that it is necessarily true, because of multicollinearity between the independent variables. For example, while there may be a high correlation between depreciation and physical deterioration, it may be incorrect to conclude that deterioration is important as a cause of depreciation. It may be that buildings subject to high deterioration are also likely to suffer from a poor internal specification, so that internal specification is therefore highly correlated with physical deterioration, and that internal specification is a very important predictor of depreciation. Physical deterioration will therefore be strongly correlated with depreciation but only as a result of the indirect link via internal specification. Again, poor configuration may lead to less expenditure to address physical deterioration, and the relative importance of these qualities may thereby be disguised.

This is a considerable problem in this research. There are high correlations between all independent variables, as Table 27 shows.

Table 27: Correlation between independent variables (sample: 125)

	Internal specification	External appearance	Physical deterioration
Configuration	0.686	0.501	0.565
Internal specification		0.617	0.791
External appearance			0.672

The effect of these figures is to suggest very high multicollinearity of variables. This is the result either of the existence of *good* and *bad* buildings, or of a failure of the research to adequately distinguish between qualities. Whichever is the case, it produces problems when using statistical techniques to rank building qualities.

Such a means of ranking building qualities is presented by multiple regression analysis. It is possible to use this method to construct an equation which relates the dependent variable (depreciation) to the four independent variables. It is then possible to compare the relative importance in the equation of each of these four variables.

A multiple regression model is an explanatory model, as its purpose is to identify those factors which have impacted the most on the dependant variable. Greater explanatory power will be produced by adding further variables, but this is at the cost of multicollinearity and ease of use. In addition, the model may form the basis of a predictive model which, given information about the value of independent variables, will estimate the value of the dependant variables.

Given this, the model needs to be efficient. Efficiency (not used with its strict econometric meaning) for these purposes means a combination of accuracy and predictive power (a high coefficient of determination, or $\bar{R}^2$), and a low number of significant independent variables. The method used throughout this chapter is to produce an initial explanatory equation utilising all four quality variables, and to attempt to increase the efficiency of the equation where appropriate for possible predictive use, by dropping unimportant variables.

The initial multiple regression equation is as shown in Equation 1. The value of the constant in this equation, -0.0658 (just over 6 pence) is effectively a measure of error in this equation, or at least of *noise*, or imperfect data. The value of the constant should ideally be zero, because nil depreciation should be predicted for a building scoring 5 in all four building qualities. In such a case, the values of a_1, a_2, a_3 and a_4 would be zero, and the constant represents the total value of the right hand side.

Nonetheless, a constant of 0.0658 against a prime ERV of £40.25 represents a variation (from the *correct* value) of only 0.16%, and can therefore be regarded as a satisfactory result. It is not significantly different from zero.

Equation 1: Total depreciation in ERV, all buildings (sample: 125)

Total depreciation in ERV = 0.0658 + 0.199a_1 + 0.213a_2 + 0.154a_3 + 0.103a_4

---

where a_1 = 5 - configuration score, and t = 3.93
            a_2 = 5 - internal specification score, and t = 3.86
            a_3 = 5 - external appearance score, and t = 3.82
            a_4 = 5 - physical deterioration score, and t = 2.01

$$\bar{R}^2 = 73.0\%$$

The shortfall in rent is related to the shortfall in quality, which leads to an expectation of positive relationships, and again the result is satisfactory because all signs are as intuitively expected. Depreciation is positively related with the shortfall in score of each variable: thus the lower the score, the greater the depreciation, as expected. The coefficient of determination is 73%, which easily beats the 39% explanatory power of age as an explanation of depreciation, supporting a major hypothesis in this research.

Of equal interest is the relative importance of each variable. A t-test measures significance at stated confidence levels. At the 95% level (that is, with a 5% chance that the result is accidental), a t-value of 1.96 is acceptable and this test therefore shows all four variables to be significant at that level of confidence.   Judgements of relative importance therefore rest upon the constant or coefficient for each variable. Given that the constant is close to zero as expected, a building with a score of 5 for each variable would suffer negligible or no depreciation.   Of the four variables, internal specification is most important at 0.213; configuration is second at 0.199; external appearance is third at 0.154; and physical deterioration is least important at 0.103.

This produces an important preliminary conclusion.   Of the twin causes of building depreciation, building obsolescence (as represented by shortfalls in internal specification, external appearance and configuration) appears to be much more important than physical deterioration. Investment decisions might therefore pay little attention to anticipated physical deterioration; building obsolescence is much more important.   Given that building obsolescence by its very nature (it is not directly related to use, the action of the elements or the passage of time) is difficult or impossible to predict, flexibility in terms of internal specification, external appearance and configuration is to be aimed for. It may be possible to be more specific if and when the three factors can be reduced in number. This is considered below.

Curable and incurable depreciation

A distinction commonly made by US commentators is between curable and incurable obsolescence or depreciation (see Chapter 4). For the purposes of this research, it is necessary to be specific. Following Chapter 4, *building depreciation* may be curable or incurable. More specifically again, some aspects of both *physical deterioration* and *building obsolescence* may be corrected, while other aspects may not.

This distinction can usefully be related to the four building qualities which were identified in Chapter 5 and have already been used in the analysis in this chapter. Configuration is a factor which creates wholly incurable depreciation; on the other hand, internal specification, external appearance and physical deterioration each contribute both to curable and incurable depreciation. The distinction is an important one. Incurable depreciation is a greater problem than curable depreciation; it increases property investment risk by a greater amount. Yet some appraisal solutions (for example, Sykes 1984b) ignore the distinction and (more importantly) practically ignore incurable depreciation (see Chapter 3). Is incurable depreciation *de minimis*? This is examined in this section.

Many of the buildings in the sample would have been refurbished by the freeholder or long leaseholder if vacant possession could have been obtained. A higher rent might thereby have been achieved. When a building has been newly refurbished in this way it is a reasonable conclusion that much of the curable depreciation will be stripped away, or cured. By estimating the increased rent that might be obtained, a comparison of the relative importance of curable and incurable depreciation in the sample can be estimated. This is established by relating three variables: the prime rent of £40.25; the ERV of the subject building as refurbished to a degree that was economically justified; and the actual (smoothed) ERV of the building.

The valuation panel was therefore asked to produce a consensus view of the increased rent that would be obtainable for each building following a refurbishment. This rent was again smoothed to remove siting differences. The buildings were also re-scored in terms of the curable depreciation factors of internal specification, external appearance and deterioration in order that both curable and incurable depreciation might be related to building quality in terms of the degree of curable and incurable problems suffered by each subject property. Valuers were asked to envisage the new standard of the building as refurbished, and to assess new scores for each building quality in that state. In some cases the score increased; in others it did not, suggesting an *incurable* defect. This requires a definition of an *economically justified* refurbishment. The test which valuers were requested to keep in mind was based on the assumption that unrestricted access to the building could be gained by a freeholder who would be able to carry out any improvement, subject only to that improvement adding at least as much as its cost to the value of the property.

The result is a total of three explanatory multiple regression models. These are:

Model 1

| total depreciation | = | prime rent | − | actual smoothed rent |
| | | (A) | | (B) |

$$A - B = a + b_1x_1 + b_2x_2 + b_3x_3 + b_4x_4$$

---

where a = intercept constant
  x_1 = 5 − configuration score
  x_2 = 5 − internal specification score
  x_3 = 5 − external appearance score
  x_4 = 5 − deterioration score

Model 2

| incurable depreciation | = | prime rent | − | refurbished smoothed rent |
| | | (A) | | (C) |

$$A - C = c + d_1y_1 + d_2y_2 + d_3y_3 + d_4y_4$$

---

where c = intercept constant
  y_1 = 5 − configuration score
  y_2 = 5 − refurbished internal specification score
  y_3 = 5 − refurbished external appearance score
  y_4 = 5 − refurbished deterioration score

Model 3

| curable depreciation | = | refurbished smoothed rent | − | actual smoothed rent |
| | | (C) | | (B) |

$$C - B = e + f_1z_1 + f_2z_2 + f_3z_3$$

---

where e = intercept constant
  z_1 = refurbished internal specification score − internal specification score
  z_2 = refurbished external appearance score − external appearance score
  z_3 = refurbished deterioration score − deterioration score

---

Equation 1 has been fully considered above. Equation 2 is considered immediately below, while Equation 3 is dealt with later in this section.

Incurable depreciation

For all buildings the equation is as shown below (Equation 2).

All the signs are correct, and the intercept is insignificantly different from zero as expected. Of the four variables only configuration (y_1) is significant, and is most important in determining incurable depreciation.

Equation 2: Incurable depreciation in ERV (sample: 125)

Incurable depreciation in ERV = $-0.0117 + 0.134y_1 + 0.101y_2 + 0.0801y_3 + 0.101y_4$

---

where $y_1 = 5 -$ configuration score, and $t = 3.68$
$y_2 = 5 -$ refurbished internal specification score, and $t = 1.58$
$y_3 = 5 -$ refurbished external appearance score, and $t = 1.89$
$y_4 = 5 -$ refurbished deterioration score, and $t = 1.62$

$$\bar{R}^2 = 38.7\%$$

From these results it is possible to conclude that configuration is the most important cause of incurable depreciation. It is the only significant variable. This is as expected: all other building qualities are to some extent curable.

Curable depreciation

Configuration is the only significant cause of incurable depreciation. It is not a factor in curable depreciation, as nothing can be done about it in normal circumstances. Hence curable depreciation is a function of shortfalls in internal specification, external appearance and deterioration. A measure of the relative importance of these as causes of curable depreciation is now attempted.

The results are shown in Equation 3.

Equation 3: Curable depreciation in ERV (sample: 125)

Curable depreciation in ERV = $0.0061 + 0.327z_1 + 0.0578z_2 + 0.0813z_3$

---

where $z_1 = $ refurb'd internal spec'n score $-$ internal spec'n score, and $t = 7.43$
$z_2 = $ refurb'd external appearance score $-$ external appearance score, and $t = 1.63$
$z_3 = $ refurb'd deterioration score $-$ deterioration score, and $t = 1.72$

$$\bar{R}^2 = 77.8\%$$

The coefficient of determination ($\bar{R}^2$) is around 78%, suggesting high explanatory power. All signs are as expected, and the intercept constant is negligible and insignificant, which is again a positive factor. The only significant and by far the most important variable is internal specification (z_1).

To conclude the only generally significant variable determining incurable depreciation is configuration, while the only significant variable determining curable depreciation is internal specification.

Relative importance of curable and incurable depreciation

Comparing the relative importance of curable and incurable depreciation is of some interest. Expressed as a percentage of the prime rent of £40.25, the average total depreciation in the sample of 125 and of the constituent original buildings and refurbishments may be measured and allocated to curable and incurable depreciation. The method used was as follows.

Each building was assigned three values: the prime rent of £40.25, defined as the best rent achievable for any building in the sample in the absence of any depreciation (A); the actual ERV, smoothed to exclude the effect of site differences (C); and the smoothed ERV as refurbished to an economically justifiable degree (B). The average value for all these was calculated. The results are as shown in Table 28.

Table 28: Average curable and incurable depreciation

	Prime rent (A) £	(Smoothed) average ERV refurb'd (B) £	%	actual (C) £	%	Average depreciation curable (B – C) £	%	incurable (A – B) £	%	total (A – C) £	%
All buildings	40.25	36.26	90.09	32.36	80.40	3.90	9.69	3.99	9.91	7.89	19.60
Original buildings	40.25	36.98	91.88	32.45	80.62	4.53	11.26	3.27	8.12	7.80	19.38
Refurbishments	40.25	35.73	88.77	32.24	80.10	3.49	8.67	4.52	11.23	8.01	19.90

The average total depreciation for all buildings as a percentage of the prime rent is 19.60%. This is divided roughly equally between curable depreciation (9.69%) and incurable depreciation (9.91%). However, for original buildings the total average depreciation of 19.38% is divided in favour of curable depreciation (11.26%) while for refurbishments incurable depreciation is dominant (11.23% out of 19.90%). Original buildings appear, therefore, to be more flexible than already refurbished buildings in terms of the ability to refurbish to cure depreciation. Even though economic circumstances may not, at a given time, combine to make refurbishment economically viable, a building that has not been refurbished before is less risky a proposition, on average, as it is more likely to be flexible in terms of its building qualities. Refurbishments, on the other hand, suffering more from outdated configuration, are more prone to attack by (in particular) obsolescence, which is almost impossible to anticipate. They are less flexible and therefore more risky.

A two-variable model

The analysis of curable and incurable depreciation has enabled a relatively simple explanation of building depreciation to emerge. It was concluded early in this chapter that certain building qualities, or more specifically the degree to which a building falls short of a current standard in terms of these qualities, provide a better explanation and arguably a better determinant of building depreciation than age. This was shown in Equation 1, with a coefficient of determination ($\overline{R}\wedge 2$) of 73%, compared with an $\overline{R}\wedge 2$ value of 39% for age as a determinant of depreciation.

The $\overline{R}\wedge 2$ of a four-variable model should not strictly be compared with that of a single-variable model because the coefficient of determination of depreciation would be expected to increase as variables are added to the equation. However, as variables are added the model becomes less easy to interpret and use. A suitable compromise may be reached, whereby fewer variables may still provide a model with high explanatory power.

Of the four variables, physical deterioration was least important in Equation 1, which showed internal specification and configuration to be most important. A separate study of incurable depreciation showed the only significant variable for all buildings to be configuration; a separate study of curable depreciation showed the only significant variable for all buildings to be internal specification. Given the existence of multicollinearity in the model, a combination of configuration and internal specification suggests itself as a potentially efficient two-variable model.

The following chain of logic produces a two-variable model. Total depreciation is made up of incurable depreciation and curable depreciation. The major and only significant cause of incurable depreciation is shortfall in configuration. The major and only significant cause of curable depreciation is shortfall in internal specification. Total depreciation is thus primarily a function of shortfall in configuration and shortfall in internal specification. Adding further variables will be inefficient: while explanatory power may increase, the cost of this in terms of complexity, data requirements and multicollinearity is too high. The equation produced by comparing these two significant variables with the dependent variable is therefore shown below (Equation 4).

Note that the explanatory power of this model is 67.2% compared with 73.0% (Equation 1) for the four-variable model and 38.8% for age against depreciation (Table 24). Thus the model has close to twice the power of age as a determinant of depreciation; it is only marginally below the power of the four-variable model and (in simple terms) twice as easy to use (two variables instead of four are to be provided). It explains over two-thirds of depreciation in rental value. (The importance of these two variables is further confirmed by a survey of occupiers: see below.) Multicollinearity is reduced and the significance of variables is increased.

Equation 4: Total depreciation in ERV (sample: 125)

Total depreciation in ERV = $0.053 + 0.233a1 + 0.374a2$

---

where $a1 = 5 -$ configuration score, and $t = 4.21$
$a2 = 5 -$ internal specification score, and $t = 8.34$

$$\overline{R}^2 = 67.2\%$$

Equation 4 means that for a prime building letting at £40.25, with perfect building qualities, a one-point reduction in the configuration score (from excellent to good, as a result of changing market demand) results in a £0.23 reduction in rental value; and a one point reduction in the internal specification score reduces rental value by £0.37. Properties with a site score of less than five will see this differential reduced by the smoothing factor, for example to £0.22 and £0.36 where the property has a site score of 4. (However, this type of reasoning cannot be taken very far, as problems with non-normally distributed data and multicollinearity result in an *explanation* which is dangerously inaccurate in *prediction*. For example, the lowest rental made possible by this equation is close to the mean rental for the sample and is therefore erroneously high.)

This cross-section rent analysis is the major attempt in this research to relate depreciation to rental value. It will, later in this chapter, be combined with a cross-section yield analysis (Section 5) to produce a cross-section capital value analysis (Section 6). Before proceeding to complete the cross-section analysis, however, two checks on the findings of the rent study are described. The first is a longitudinal rent analysis (Section 3); the second is a survey of occupiers (Section 4). These checks will enable the findings of the cross-section rent analysis to be confirmed, or otherwise.

3. Longitudinal rent analysis

Introduction

In Chapter 5 the longitudinal analysis is discussed as a means of measuring depreciation by tracking the performance of a sample of different buildings over time. It is now to be used as a means of checking the main results of the cross-section analysis described above. The objects of the analysis are:

    i to compare depreciation rates for buildings of different ages, and to test age as an indicator of depreciation; and

   ii to relate relative performance in terms of depreciation to physical deterioration and obsolescence factors.

Several potential difficulties with a longitudinal approach were identified in Chapter 5. Several of these were encountered in practice. Firstly, it is not possible to hold site factors constant over time. Certain sections of a location will improve while others decline due to environmental obsolescence and the impact of supply and demand shifts. The impact of this impurity in this study of depreciation has been minimised by tight definition of a study area which is unlikely to have been subject to large variations of this type. However, some marginal changes are possible.

Secondly, it was stated that it is difficult to find a large data sample with evidence of performance, which has to include rental values, yields and expenditures, over a period. This was certainly true in this study, and became a problem which dictated the exclusion of some data. The difficulty of tracing building expenditure was avoided by dropping any building which had been subject to expenditure over the study period. Also, no attempt was made to include yields in the study due to suspicions of reduced accuracy of the data collected in respect of 1986 yields (see Section 5 below) which are likely to be exacerbated for any point in the past. Next, it was only possible to include properties which formed part of the 1986 sample of 125 buildings and which were also in existence at the earlier study date (1980). Finally, properties were only included in the longitudinal study where reliable evidence of mid-1980 rental value existed, this coming from two sources: the RICS/Actuaries Office Rents Index (see Chapter 5), and the records of four major investors in the market.

The effect of this data selection process was to reduce the database from 125 properties to 33. This was largely the product of excluding any building which had been built or subject to major expenditure since 1980, around 65 of the buildings having been built or refurbished over the period 1980-1986. It has to be accepted that the resulting sample of 33 is a very small base on which to carry out a meaningful analysis, and the results are unlikely to be highly significant.

The third problem in a longitudinal study of this type is that estimates of the quality of subject buildings in terms of internal specification, external appearance and configuration factors can only be retrospective. It is impossible to measure changes in the market perception of the quality of a building in these respects over the study period, but it is exactly such changes together with shifts in site quality which would be the cause of different depreciation rates. The value of a longitudinal study in explaining depreciation by its causes is therefore limited unless the study is repeated at a later date. Consequently, a full analysis relating depreciation to building qualities was rejected in favour of a more restricted study.

Finally, the cyclical nature of the market may distort a measurement of building depreciation, and the research is critically dependent upon the choice of data points. 1980 was selected as a neutral point in the market for this purpose, because recent high levels of growth had tailed off and future poor performance of the property was yet to come. 1986 may be seen in retrospect to have been the final year of a bear market. The result may be higher than normal depreciation rates.

In the light of these difficulties, the data collected comprised the estimated rental values as at mid-1980 for 33 buildings from the database of 125 which had not been subject to major expenditure (greater than 15% of estimated annual rental value in any one year) since 1980. Where owners supplied data, March or July valuations were accepted; where the RICS/Actuaries Rent Index was used, the July valuation was taken.

Age against depreciation in ERV

Depreciation in estimated rental values over the study period 1980 to 1986 was measured as follows. Firstly, the prime or top rent from the 1986 sample (£40.25) and the 1980 sample (£22.27) were compared to show a prime rate of rental growth of 10.37% per annum over a six year study period. Secondly, actual rates of rental growth for all 33 properties in the sample were calculated. Some properties produced rental growth which exceeded the prime rate, but the average was lower at 9.59% per annum. Thirdly, average rental depreciation was calculated. Depreciation is defined for the purpose of this analysis as the difference between the rate of growth in prime properties (10.37%) and the actual rate of growth in each subject property. Average depreciation suffered was therefore 0.78% per annum over the period 1980 - 1986. Some buildings showed negative depreciation on this basis, but this need not be a major concern (growth started from a lower base, or site quality improved, for example).

Actual depreciation rates were then related to age. The correlation coefficient is positive at $r = 0.207$, suggesting that an acceleration of depreciation has occurred. Old buildings have depreciated more quickly, although the relationship is a tenuous one. (A t-test shows that this result is not significant at the 95% confidence level: given the small sample, it may be the result of chance. This is a common difficulty in this longitudinal study).

A clearer picture is shown in Table 29 below, which relates depreciation rates to age at 1980. Inconsistency in the age grouping is the product of a small data sample.

Table 29: Depreciation rate against age at 1980 (sample: 33)

Age at 1980	Number in sample	Dep'n rate pa (%)
0 - 3	13	0.41
5 - 12	13	0.69
18 +	7	1.91

These results illustrate the positive correlation coefficient relating age at 1980 to depreciation rate per annum. Depreciation is greater for older buildings; more specifically, depreciation is slight in the early years and increases at an exponential rate. In Table 29 above the depreciation rate for seven buildings of ages 5 to 7 years within the second age band is low, at 0.41% per annum, accelerating to 1.33% per annum for the remaining six properties of age 8 to 12 years. Thus it is possible to conclude that depreciation is slight over years 0 to 7, accelerates thereafter and reaches a much higher rate after year 18.

This broadly confirms the findings of the cross-section study reported in Section 2 above. Table 25 showed that depreciation is at its height by a considerable margin over years 17 to 26. Table 30 below compares cross-section and longitudinal results. (In the longitudinal results, note that age is expressed as a range of the average ages of the subject properties over the period 1980 - 1986.)

Although it is difficult to be precise, the longitudinal study appears to confirm the major finding of the cross-section age study, which is that depreciation strikes hardest after the third and/or fourth rent reviews.

Building qualities against depreciation in ERV

As stated above, it would be a mistake to go into detail regarding the effect of different building qualities upon depreciation rates over the study period in a longitudinal analysis. Firstly, the sample is small and results are not likely to be statistically significant. Secondly, building qualities have been appraised at 1986 and a meaningful analysis could be produced only by relating depreciation rate to change in building quality as perceived in the market over the study period.

Nonetheless, a simple study has been attempted. Each of five building qualities (including siting) at 1986 has been related to the annual depreciation rate over the 1980 - 1986 period using simple regression analysis. Results are as shown in Table 31. Note that siting is included as a quality: the rental values are therefore unsmoothed.

Table 30: Depreciation rate and age: comparison of cross-section and longitudinal results

Cross-section		Longitudinal	
Age	Dep'n rate pa (%)	Age	Dep'n rate pa (%)
2-7	0.977	1-7	0.41
7-11	0.615	8-14	0.69
11-17	0.496	18-24	1.91
17-26	1.785		
26-34	0.336		

Table 31: Building quality and depreciation: a longitudinal analysis (sample: 33)

Independent variable	Coefficient of correlation (r)	Coefficient of determination ($\overline{R}^2$)	Significance (t value)
Siting	+ 0.0499	0.249%	0.28
Configuration	− 0.2394	5.730%	− 1.37
Internal specification	− 0.2751	7.570%	− 1.59
External appearance	− 0.0428	0.183%	− 0.28
Deterioration	− 0.1467	2.150%	− 0.83

It must be stated that none of these results is statistically significant at the 95% confidence level; that is, there is more than a 5% probability that these results are pure chance. For example, the better sites at 1986 appear to have shown *greater* depreciation over the 1980 to 1986 period. This is contrary to expectation, but the relationship is so slight and the result so insignificant in a statistical sense that it should be rejected as meaningless.

Of the four building qualities, all show the expected relationship. The poorer the building in terms of these qualities in 1986, the greater has been the depreciation over 1980 to 1986. This only makes sense alongside the implication that poor quality in 1986 indicates an increase in importance of that quality and/or the likelihood that quality has deteriorated over the study period. This is realistic and is confirmed by a positive correlation between age and depreciation rate although differential movements in quality will reduce the significance and reliability of this information.

An interesting result of the longitudinal study is the ranking of internal specification and configuration as the most significant causes of depreciation in rental values. This replicates and confirms the findings of the cross-section study. Equation 4 showed the two-variable model which was suggested as the most efficient predictor of depreciation in rental value. The two variables were internal specification and configuration, in that order. Given an assumption that poor configuration and internal specification scores indicate the likelihood of a deterioration in the market perception of the building in terms of these qualities over the study period and/or an increase in their importance, it can be stated that these factors are confirmed by the longitudinal study to be of prime importance in explaining the rental depreciation of central City office buildings. This is also confirmed by an occupier survey (see Section 4 below).

Conclusions

The deficiencies of a longitudinal study in testing variables which impact upon rent are set out in Chapter 5 and in this section (above). In this particular case, the sample size is small and the results were unlikely to be highly significant, as was proven to be the case.

Nonetheless, two tentative but major findings, each confirming the results of the cross-section rent analysis, emerge. These are as follows.

1. Rental depreciation strikes hardest after the third or fourth review.
2. Internal specification and configuration deficiencies, in that order, are the two predominant causes of rental depreciation in central City office buildings.

4. A survey of occupiers

Introduction

Quite apart from the usual questioning of the degree to which extrapolation of a positivist empirical analysis is meaningful, several criticisms of the analysis which forms the basis of this chapter and therefore much of this research may perhaps be made. Firstly, the choice of four building qualities and siting as the predominant factors affecting rental value, albeit the result of a brainstorming session conducted by the researchers with the participation of four previously briefed and prepared expert City office agents, may be said to be subjective to those agents and not necessarily representative of the views of the office occupiers and intending office occupiers they purported to simulate. Consequently the research may be flawed as it fails to relate depreciation to the building qualities that are really important in the market.

Secondly, given the problems of multicollinearity which inevitably exist in a study of this type, can the researchers be sure that the ranking of importance of building qualities thrown out by multiple regression analysis reflects the importance assigned to those variables by occupiers? Alternatively, are the results statistically significant but practically misleading?

A third possible problem is the potential charge that the analysis is not sufficiently wide. It is beyond question that further research is necessary to explore the sub-factors which together make up deterioration and obsolescence. For example, it may be useful to know that internal specification is the most important factor in terms of causes of rental depreciation, but what are the most important factors within internal specification?

Finally, can the researcher be sure that the agents who constituted the valuation panel were correct in the assignation of appraisals to each of the 125 buildings, or do occupiers have a markedly different view?

A survey of 316 occupiers of the 125 buildings in the data sample was carried out in December 1986. The response rate was average, around 25% of those questioned returning correctly completed forms. The data sample is 80 respondents, a number which is arguably acceptable for the purposes of analysis.

Choice of building qualities

The office agents who took part in the first brainstorming session established a list of the four qualities of a building which were considered to be of greatest importance in determining rental value. These are fully defined and described in Appendix B. These qualities were: configuration, internal specification, external appearance and deterioration.

To confirm whether or not these are indeed the factors which actual or prospective City office occupiers take into account in renting space and, by implication, in determining rental value, the occupiers of the subject 125 buildings were asked to state any factors not included in the list of five which they felt to be of particular importance.

Eighteen (22.5% of the total) chose to list extra factors. However, many of these were merely sub-factors of the five qualities. For example, *raised access floors, symmetrical building configuration, raised modular floors, large open floor*, and *constructional suitability for dealing room environment* were quoted, but all fall within the configuration quality. Similarly, *good adaptable services, 24-hour air-conditioning* and *air-conditioning independent to each floor* stated by some respondents all fall within the quality of internal specification. *Proximity to markets/associated business/professional advisers* were all seen as important, but are siting factors, excluded from the analysis.

The only factors which are additional to the list of five qualities which emerged from the survey were *security* (once), *availability of car parking spaces* (twice) and *large quantity of space on one site* (twice).

Given these results it is concluded that the use of the original five factors in the analysis does not omit any important factors as perceived in the market for City office space, and the agents' choice of variables was a correct reflection of occupiers' preferences and priorities. No modification of the original research method was therefore necessary.

Ranking of building qualities

The rental analysis carried out by cross-section and tentatively confirmed by the longitudinal study placed internal specification and configuration clearly ahead as the two most important building qualities affecting rental depreciation. Deterioration was shown in the cross-section study to be least important, confirming the importance of obsolescence, represented by configuration and the remaining two qualities, in determining depreciation.

In order to check this, occupiers of the subject properties were asked to rank the importance of the four building qualities using a scale of one to five. A score of one was awarded for high importance. The building quality with the lowest total score is therefore the most important to the sample of 80 occupiers.

Results are shown in Table 32 and confirm the ordering produced by multiple regression analysis with the exception of the reversal in importance of configuration and internal specification. These two factors are clearly ahead, and they were also isolated as being the two most significant qualities in the two variable model represented by Equation 4, so the reversal is not problematic and statistical and hierarchical ordering approaches can be said to be broadly consistent in this case.

Table 32: Occupiers' ranking of building qualities

Quality	Total score	Rank
Configuration	191.0	1
Internal specification	236.5	2
External appearance	289.5	3
Deterioration	299.0	4

However, their reversal is of interest in the light of the distinction between curable and incurable depreciation pursued in Section 2. Configuration is of unique importance in determining incurable depreciation; internal specification, on the other hand, is the major predictor of curable depreciation. Tenants may pay less rent for buildings which are poor in either respect; but they may well regard configuration as the greater problem because they can do little about it. Internal specification can be and is improved by the tenants under the terms of full repairing and insuring leases.

The results were split into responses from banking and non-banking related occupiers in order to test the relative importance of configuration to each group. The initial ranking was repeated in both cases but the gap between configuration and internal specification was increased in the banking analysis. This confirmed an expectation that banking-related occupation placed more of a premium upon configuration.

This survey may be regarded as a significant confirmation of the results of the cross-section and longitudinal rent analyses described above. Internal specification and configuration are of superior importance in determining rental depreciation; physical deterioration is least important.

Building qualities: an analysis of sub-factors

In order to explore further the importance of building qualities in determining rental value, and hence depreciation in rental value, an attempt was made to proceed to a second level of building quality analysis. Figure 1 (Chapter 4) shows that the three obsolescence factors may be further broken down into two sub-factors each. Deterioration may also be split, into interior and exterior deterioration.

Occupiers of the subject buildings were asked to indicate which of the two sub-factors within each quality was the most important. Table 33 shows the results: clear preferences in each category. As a consequence of these findings, illustrated in Figure 7, a further analysis of configuration on the basis of floor layout only was carried out; this was found to be of some interest (see Baum, 1989). No further analysis of these findings was carried out, but it is possible to offer a tentative conclusion that, given the importance of configuration and internal specification, and the clear preference of sub-factors within each, the two most significant predictors of rental depreciation are shortfalls in floor layout and the quality and quantity of services provided.

Occupiers' appraisals

Occupiers were asked to rate the quality of their space on a scale of 1 to 5 in terms of the four building qualities and siting in order that the appraisals of the valuation panel might be compared with the occupiers' own appraisals.

For individual buildings there were many disagreements; on average, they were insignificant. Table 34 shows the results of a comparison of agents' and occupiers' appraisals of the buildings. Occupiers' scores are the average and standard deviation of all responses; agents' scores are the average and standard deviation of appraisals only for those buildings where occupiers provided scores.

Table 33: Importance of building sub-factors

Factor	Sub-factor	Rating
Configuration	Floor layout	51 (86.4%)
	Floor-to-ceiling height	8 (13.6%)
Internal specification	Quantity/quality of services	47 (79.7%)
	Quality of finishes	12 (20.3%)
External appearance	Impact of entrance hall, etc	44 (72.1%)
	Quality of external design	17 (27.9%)
Deterioration	Deterioration of interior	41 (65.1%)
	Deterioration of exterior	22 (34.9%)

Table 34: Agents' and occupiers' appraisals compared

	Average of scores of:		Standard deviation of scores of:	
	agents	occupiers	agents	occupiers
Configuration	2.78	3.13	0.796	1.038
Internal specification	3.04	3.25	0.983	1.016
External appearance	3.33	3.49	0.994	0.903
Deterioration	3.10	3.53	1.003	0.848
Siting	3.58	4.38	0.860	0.668

Table 34 shows occupiers to be consistently more positive, as would be expected from those who have a subjective interest against those forming an objective comparative view. The largest difference is in the siting score; perhaps occupiers are less able than valuers to distinguish micro location factors from the overall location effect of the central City, as supported by a low standard deviation for the occupiers' site score. The ranking of external appearance and deterioration is reversed in terms of average scores; others are confirmed.

Figure 7: Occupiers' assessments of the importance of building qualities

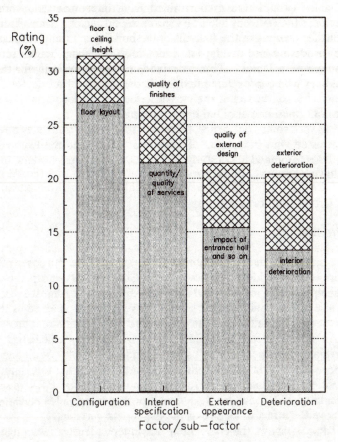

Valuers acting as proxies for occupiers exhibit a bias. However, because that bias appears to be consistent the agents' appraisals, being relative, can be taken as indicative of the market view.

Conclusions

The survey of occupiers was particularly important in three respects. Firstly, it gave support to the selection of building qualities which appear to have been correctly determined and to have reflected the views of the market among occupiers. Secondly, the ranking of qualities as predictors of depreciation was confirmed: deterioration is least important and internal specification and configuration are most important. Hence a hierarchical approach confirmed the statistical approach. The reversal of internal specification and configuration from the statistical analysis ordering may be explained by the degree to which occupiers are constrained from improving upon configuration, which thereby takes on greater importance for them. Thirdly, a further analysis of the four qualities shows clear results, especially the predominance of layout over floor-to-ceiling height in the configuration factor. This prompted a further analysis of configuration which concentrated upon the more important sub-factor. The conclusions of the rental analyses described in Sections 2 and 3 above are confirmed and clarified by the occupier survey.

It is with some confidence, therefore, that these results may now be contrasted with the results of a study of yields, and the two sets of analyses combined into a study of depreciation in capital values, in the following sections of this chapter.

5. Cross-section yield analysis

Introduction

The process of data collection and appraisal for the purposes of the cross-section yield study is described in Chapter 5. To recap, the data available are the market yield for each building as at August 1986; the lot size of each building; the smoothed yield, based on an adjustment for lot size; and all other data used in the cross-section rent analysis.

As a first step, these data were analysed by calculating the correlations between the adjusted dependent variable (yield) and the independent variable(s) of, first, age and, second, the four building qualities plus siting. The correlation between yield and ERV was also calculated. The analyses were then repeated using yields adjusted to remove the effect of lot size as the dependent variable.

Table 35 shows the correlations for independent variables against yield and smoothed yield. Note the smoothing effect, which is to almost completely erase correlations between size and yield and to increase all other correlations significantly. In the case of configuration, an incorrect sign is reversed.

Yield and size against depreciation in ERV

The correlation coefficient between yield and ERV is -0.305. A negative correlation is expected, as a high rent indicates an attractive proposition for investors who pay a high price and accept a low yield. High rent therefore correlates negatively with low yield. 0.3 is, however, quite low, and it is apparent that lot size has a considerable impact upon this value. The relationship between smoothed yield and ERV, on the other hand, is much higher at -0.635. This is more in line with expectations, although it does leave room for a conclusion that factors influencing yield are not of identical impact on ERV. For example, it has already been seen (in Chapter 5) that site is of much less impact on yield than on ERV. Other differences will be explored below.

Table 35: Correlation of variables against yield and smoothed yield (sample: 125)

Variable	Yield correlation	Smoothed yield correlation
Size	− 0.593	0.002
ERV	− 0.305	− 0.635
Configuration	0.015	− 0.369
Internal specification	− 0.330	− 0.617
External appearance	− 0.325	− 0.532
Siting	− 0.189	− 0.415
Deterioration	− 0.357	− 0.587
Age	0.389	0.546

Table 36 below shows the correlation matrix between yield, size and ERV and building qualities. This enables a fuller check of the relationships between variables to be made.

Table 36: Correlation matrix: yield, size and ERV against building qualities (sample: 125)

	Yield	Size	Smoothed yield	ERV	Smoothed ERV
Size	− 0.593				
Smoothed Yield	0.789	0.002			
ERV	− 0.305	− 0.346	− 0.635		
Smoothed ERV	− 0.304	− 0.342	− 0.627	0.988	
Configuration	0.015	− 0.514	− 0.369	0.700	0.702
Internal specification	− 0.330	− 0.292	− 0.617	0.772	0.794
External appearance	− 0.325	− 0.186	− 0.532	0.685	0.693
Siting	− 0.189	− 0.229	− 0.415	0.636	0.520
Deterioration	− 0.357	− 0.224	− 0.587	0.710	0.741
Age	0.389	0.111	− 0.546	− 0.588	− 0.623

An unexpected relationship is that which exists between size and ERV, for which the correlation coefficient is -0.346. Given that estimates of value per square foot were provided for hypothetical units of 10,000 square feet, there should simplistically be no correlation between size and ERV. However, note that there is a negative correlation between size and all building qualities, especially configuration. This suggests that smaller buildings are badly configured, and are also of reduced quality in external appearance and so on. Hence the relationship between size and ERV is indirect, and not necessarily the problem it appears to be.

Small lots may be attractive to investors, hence the low yields assigned to them. There is, however, a trade-off in terms of reduced attractiveness in plan layout. This may explain the tiny increase in average yield from 5.23% to 5.25% for buildings below 10,000 square feet (see Chapter 5) and suggests an optimal size of 10,000 to 20,000 square feet.

Age against depreciation in yield

There is a less pronounced relationship between yield and age ($r = 0.389$) than between ERV and age ($r = -0.588$). When the effect of size is taken out by smoothing, however, the correlation between age and yield increases to 0.546, close to the corresponding figure for ERV (smoothed for site quality) and age (0.623). The result is as expected, with a positive and fairly strong correlation between age and yield (as age increases, yield increases). This will contribute to a negative correlation between capital value and age (see Section 6 below).

The regression equation for (depreciation in) smoothed yield against age is shown in Table 37 below (compare this with Table 24, an equivalent table showing depreciation in smoothed ERV against age).

Table 37: Age against yield

No of properties	125
Mean age	9.62
Mean smoothed yield (%)	5.23
Mean depreciation (yield: %)*	0.97
Standard deviation (yield: %)	0.54
Regression equation: Depreciation (%) =	0.19 + 0.031 age
Coefficient of correlation (r)	0.541
Coefficient of determination ($\overline{R}^2$) (%)	29.27
Significance (t)	7.23

Note: * against prime property, building code number 96: 4.75%

A comparison of Table 24 and Table 37 demonstrates that higher correlations exist between smoothed ERV and age than between smoothed yield and age.

Table 38 (illustrated by Figure 8) shows the behaviour of yield against age for grouped data for all buildings.

Table 38: Depreciation in yield and age band (sample: 125)

Age	Frequency	Mean age	Average smoothed yield	Index	Dep'n rate pa (%)	Years
0-4	48	1.94	5.016	100		
5-9	31	6.77	5.085	98.64	0.282	2-7
10-14	19	11.26	5.241	95.71	0.653	7-11
15-19	10	16.70	5.643	88.89	1.254	11-17
20-29	8	26.13	5.914	84.82	0.432	17-26
30 +	9	34.44	5.815	86.26	+0.173	26-34

Mean annual depreciation rate: 0.42%

Figure 8: Age bands and depreciation* in yields

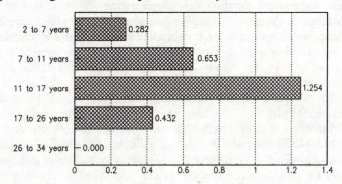

Note: * depreciation expressed as % per annum

As Figure 8 shows, the major impact of depreciation upon yield for the average of all buildings in the data sample strikes over years 11 to 17, while the major impact upon rental value occurred at years 17-26. The conclusion remaining is the relative resistance of City office buildings to depreciation over the first 10 years of their lives, and the possibility that on average yields accurately discount depreciation in rents.

Building qualities against depreciation in yield

The relationship of (depreciation in) yield and building qualities is less clear than the relationship of (depreciation in) rental value and building qualities. Individual correlations are compared below in Table 39.

Table 39: Building qualities, yields and ERV: correlations (sample: 125)

	(Depreciation in)	
	smoothed ERV	smoothed yield
Internal specification	0.794	– 0.617
Physical deterioration	0.741	– 0.587
Configuration	0.702	– 0.369
External appearance	0.693	– 0.532

The effect of siting differences remains within the yield data, but smoothing this factor away would be of little impact (in fact a test showed that the correlations fall). The most noticeable change between ERV and yield data is the considerably reduced importance of configuration for investors, and the increased relative importance of external appearance and physical deterioration.

Multiple regression analysis is again used to identify the important building qualities explaining yield depreciation. Multicollinearity between the four qualities (see Table 27) has again to be borne in mind as a problem in the following model (Equation 5). Depreciation, defined as the actual smoothed yield minus the prime yield of 4.75%, is again related to the shortfall in each score; the relationships should therefore be positive. The intercept constant should be small.

Of interest in Equation 5 is the reduced explanatory power (the $\bar{R}^2$ of 41.8% compares to 73.0% for depreciation in ERV against building qualities), the intercept (statistically insignificant, as hoped, but more important at 3% of the prime yield than the rent intercept in Equation 1) and the sign reversal for configuration. The latter appears to suggest that the yield increases as configuration improves, which is of course the opposite of the expected result. The cause of this problem is in two parts. Firstly, there is a low correlation between yield (which is the same as yield depreciation in statistical terms) and configuration (Table 36 shows this to be easily the lowest of the correlation coefficients for the four qualities at -0.369); secondly, multicollinearity between the four qualities may have caused the sign reversal.

Equation 5: Depreciation in smoothed yield (sample: 125)

Depreciation in smoothed yield = $0.147 - 0.095a_1 + 0.248a_2 + 0.115a_3 + 0.0899a_4$

---

where $a_1 = 5 -$ configuration score, and t $= -1.49$
        $a_2 = 5 -$ internal specification score, and t $= 3.52$
        $a_3 = 5 -$ external appearance score, and t $= 2.23$
        $a_4 = 5 -$ physical deterioration score, and t $= 1.38$

$$\bar{R}^2 = 41.8\%$$

Given that configuration is not statistically significant at the 95% confidence level, it is of dubious use as an explanation of yield depreciation. This might suggest that investors have paid little attention to it in purchasing office investments, certainly less than occupiers have concerned themselves about it in deciding to rent space. Deterioration is also insignificant.

For both occupiers and investors, shortfall in internal specification is most important as the cause of depreciation: see Section 6 below. For investors, external appearance is also important; for occupiers, this factor is replaced by configuration, represented particularly by floor layout.

Conclusions

To conclude, internal specification is the most important quality for investors. The importance of the four variables in explaining yield increases as building quality declines is much less than the corresponding importance of these variables in explaining rental value decreases, probably reflecting a more efficient market for occupation than for investment. Put another way, the first valuation panel was probably more able to place accurate rental estimates upon buildings than the second panel was able to achieve in respect of yields, and this is reflected by the number of different yields suggested compared to the number of rental values suggested (12 against 31).

Less reliance should therefore be placed upon the findings in respect of yields than upon the findings in respect of rental values.

6. Cross-section capital value analysis

Introduction

An analysis of capital values is a combination of the analyses of rental values and yields. Notional capital value is the result of dividing smoothed ERV by the respective smoothed yield in each case. The importance of age as an influence on capital value will therefore reflect the importance of age as an influence upon both rental value and yield. Similarly, the importance of the four building qualities as an influence on capital value will reflect their influence upon rental value and yield. For building owners who hold property for other than the very long term, depreciation in capital value is of more significance than depreciation in rental value or yield. It is this, coupled with rental income over the holding period, which determines return and performance. The greater the holding period, the greater the effect of rental performance; the shorter the holding period, the greater the effect of capital value changes. In Chapter 8, a 15-year holding period is adopted for analysis purposes, and within this time scale capital value change is of predominant impact.

The following analysis of capital value change across the sample at August 1986 (a cross-section analysis) examines the relative capital values of holdings of different ages and different qualities.

Capital value is quoted as the value per square foot for a building newly let in 10,000 square foot units on a standard lease to good quality tenants at August 1986. The effect of site quality on rent is removed in smoothed ERV; the effect of lot size on yield is removed in smoothed yield. Smoothed capital value is thus the capital value as above, but without the effect on yield of lot size and without the effect on rental value of site quality. The figure therefore shown is the notional value per square foot of the sample building if sold in a lot size of up to 20,000 square feet and situated upon a prime quality site.

Explaining variations, therefore, are (on a simple level) age differences and (on a second, more complex level) differences in building quality. The former relationship is explored immediately below.

Age against depreciation in capital value

The relationship of age and smoothed capital value depreciation, given by $r = 0.624$, shows that the effect of combining yield and rental value exaggerates the individual effect of age on depreciation in each ($r = 0.389$ and $r = 0.541$ respectively). The result is a relatively strong positive correlation.

The regression equation for smoothed capital value against age is as shown in Table 40, which should be compared with Tables 24 (rental value against age) and 37 (yield against age).

The importance of age in capital value depreciation is demonstrated more clearly in Table 41.

Table 40: Age against capital value

No of properties	125
Mean age (years)	9.62
Mean smoothed CV (£)	631.39
Mean depreciation in CV (£)*	307.10
Standard deviation of CV and dep'n (£)	143.01
Regression equation: Depreciation (£) =	220 + 9.24 age
Coefficient of correlation (r)	0.624
Coefficient of determination ($\overline{R}^2$) (%)	38.93
Significance (t)	8.93

Note: * against prime property, building code no 96: £938.69.

Table 41: Depreciation in capital value and age band (sample: 125)

Age	Frequency	Mean age	Mean smoothed capital value	Index	Dep'n rate pa (%)	Years
0-4	48	1.94	699.69	100		
5-9	31	6.77	660.43	94.39	1.161	2-7
10-14	19	11.26	637.37	91.09	0.735	7-11
15-19	10	16.70	568.76	81.23	1.813	11-17
20-29	8	26.13	432.48	61.81	2.059	17-26
30 +	9	34.44	423.09	60.47	0.161	26-34

Mean annual depreciation rate: 1.22%

Figure 9 shows that depreciation accelerates and becomes critical between years 11 and 26, after which it is not noticeable. Before this the greater incidence occurs in the early years, 2 to 7. It is curious that years 5 to 10 is the period identified by Salway in the CALUS study of depreciation (Salway, 1986) as the period of *greatest* depreciation in rents: this research shows it to be a period of low depreciation in both rents and capital values. The implications for an investor in buy or sell decisions will be explored in Chapter 8.

Figure 9: Age bands and depreciation* in capital values

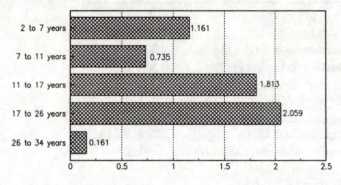

Note: * depreciation expressed as % per annum

Building quality against depreciation in capital value

Individual correlations for building qualities against (depreciation in) smoothed capital value are compared with corresponding values for rental value and yield in Table 42.

Table 42: Building qualities, yields, ERV and capital value: correlations (sample: 125)

| | (Depreciation in) smoothed | | |
	ERV	yield	CV
Configuration	0.702	– 0.369	0.638
Internal specification	0.794	– 0.617	0.789
External appearance	0.693	– 0.532	0.703
Physical deterioration	0.741	– 0.587	0.741

Correlations between capital value and building qualities are noticeably similar to the corresponding values for ERV. The effect of lower yield correlations has been largely neutral, but note the effect upon configuration, which has become noticeably less strongly correlated with depreciation.

Tables 40 and 42 show that age is inferior to individual building qualities in explaining depreciation. A correlation coefficient for age against depreciation in capital value of 0.624 ranks last in strength of correlation.

Given the relative individual correlation values, it is not surprising that the explanatory power of a multiple regression equation combining all four qualities is superior to the power of a simple regression model based upon age. For all buildings, Equation 6 shows the four variables regressed against depreciation in capital value and confirms this expectation.

Equation 6: Depreciation in capital value, all buildings (sample: 125)

Depreciation in capital value = 32.726 + 24.1a1 + 56.4a2 + 40.5a3 + 23.5a4

---

where   a1 = 5 – configuration score, and t = 2.00
            a2 = 5 – internal specification score, and t = 4.29
            a3 = 5 – external appearance score, and t = 4.21
            a4 = 5 – deterioration score, and t = 1.92

$$\bar{R}^2 = 70.6\%$$

This is an important model which confirms the importance of obsolescence as the major cause of depreciation. The first three qualities are pure obsolescence factors: see Section 2 above. All rank above depreciation in significance and in the size of the relevant constant. Deterioration is marginally insignificant at the 95% confidence level as an explanation of depreciation, and this is an even clearer indication of the relative unimportance of deterioration than Equation 1 (ERV against four qualities) suggested.

The $\bar{R}^2$ of 38.9% for age against depreciation in capital value (Table 40) should be compared with the above result. Building quality is a better explanation of depreciation than age; more specifically, building obsolescence is nearly twice as good an explanation of building depreciation than is age.

Of the four building qualities identified in this research, internal specification, or more accurately the degree to which a building falls short of the prime standard in this quality, is the best explanation of depreciation, or the degree to which capital value falls short of prime values. Second most important is external appearance; third is configuration; and within that quality it is plan layout which is of prime significance. Deterioration is, of the four qualities, least important, and is statistically insignificant in this sample of City office buildings.

Conclusions

Building quality is superior to age as an explanation of capital value depreciation. This is so even when individual correlations are compared; when building qualities are combined into multi-variate models, the difference is (not surprisingly) considerably greater.

The most important indicator of a shortfall in capital value below prime values is a shortfall in the quality of internal specification. (This is true both for original buildings and for refurbishments.) While configuration, specifically layout, is of next greatest importance to occupiers as reflected in rental value (see also Section 4), this factor is exceeded in overall importance by external appearance, which is similarly significant in its impact upon yield. Configuration is of tertiary importance, despite its predominance as a cause of incurable depreciation in rental value.

Deterioration is least significant, confirming the ascendancy of obsolescence as a cause of building depreciation.

7. Conclusions

Summary of methodology

Chapters 5 and 6 of this book describe an attempt to gauge the relative importance, and to measure the relative impact, of the forces behind depreciation. Data analysis is carried out at two levels: firstly, as a precursor to the major study, depreciation is related to building age to produce some empirical evidence for comparison with the results of the CALUS study; secondly, an attempt is made to identify and measure the causes of obsolescence and depreciation, using as a basis the classification constructed in Chapter 4. There are two sets of empirical tests: the first and major tests, which are described in this chapter, concern City offices.

Four separate data analyses were carried out. These were a cross-section rent analysis; a longitudinal rent analysis; a cross-section yield analysis; and a cross-section capital value analysis. Each was performed at the two levels referred to above. In all four analyses age is first related to depreciation, and building qualities are then related to depreciation. Certain of the findings are compared with the views of occupiers, ascertained by questionnaire, in Section 4.

Age and depreciation

There is a stronger correlation between age and depreciation for original buildings than there is for refurbishments. This applied to analyses of rent, yield and (necessarily) capital value. In summary, it was found that the City office buildings in the sample depreciated less than the CALUS average, due to higher site value content and possibly better design.

The average rate of depreciation in capital value is 1.22% per annum. Depreciation is particularly fierce between years 11 and 26. Older buildings at 1980 depreciated in rental value more quickly than newer buildings over the period 1980 to 1986. The rate increases from 0.41% per annum for buildings aged below 3 years to 1.91% per annum for buildings aged over 18 years. These values all contrast with the CALUS results, which showed a steady pattern of depreciation at around 3% per annum.

Building qualities and depreciation

In support of the major hypothesis in this research, building qualities are more strongly correlated with, and are better explanations of, depreciation than is age.

Deterioration is the least important factor in each of rental, yield and capital value depreciation. Obsolescence is therefore the more important source of depreciation. Of the three obsolescence factors, internal specification and configuration are most important in rental depreciation. This is confirmed by a cross-section rent study, a longitudinal rent study, and an occupiers' survey. Layout is by far the most important factor within configuration; floor-to-ceiling height is less important than expected. Services are the most important sub-factor within internal specification, around four times as important as internal finishes. Configuration is less important to investors, who appear to place external appearance in a higher priority position, as evidenced by the effect of building qualities upon yields. Internal specification is again most important. In capital value depreciation, internal specification, external appearance and configuration in that order are all more important than deterioration.

The prediction of depreciation therefore depends upon a prediction of the future incidence of these three sources of obsolescence. However, the nature of obsolescence (a decline in utility not directly related to use, the action of the elements or the passage of time) is that it is unpredictable and may be the instantaneous result of a technological or fashion revolution. Thus a particular air-conditioning system, a stylistic building design or a specific type of layout may suddenly become obsolete. The effect is inevitable depreciation and little can be done to avoid it.

However, the impact of obsolescence is minimised if the source can be cured. Buildings should therefore be preferred if they are *flexible* in terms of the three qualities referred to above. A revolutionary air-conditioning system may be included in an old building if it is sufficiently flexible. Similarly, certain configurations will allow flexibility of layout and external appearance may even be altered in certain buildings to suit changes in fashion. Flexibility reduces the risk of an irreversible and major reduction in the market value of a building.

Curable and incurable depreciation

Flexibility is associated with curable depreciation. Curable depreciation is most significantly caused by internal specification problems, but may also result from poor external appearance and high deterioration. Incurable depreciation, on the other hand, is caused primarily by configuration problems. The buildings which are at least risk of major depreciation are those which are least prone to the possibility of incurable depreciation, and therefore have a good – flexible – configuration, or, more specifically, plan layout.

Flexibility is a factor which should be taken fully into account in investment decision-making, and a model which allows for this is constructed in Chapter 8. Before that model is discussed, a second empirical analysis (of industrial property) is described in Chapter 7.

Chapter 7

An analysis of property investment depreciation and obsolescence 2: industrials

1. Introduction

In Chapter 3, the majority of the references discussed in the literature review concerned offices. This may be because offices appear to represent a greater proportion of the national wealth, and are more strongly represented in institutional investment portfolios (in 1988, the Investment Property Databank largely covering UK insurance funds comprised 54% offices and 10% industrials and the World Markets universe dealing largely with pension funds comprised 37% offices and 16% industrials); alternatively, it may be because depreciation and obsolescence are considered to impact upon offices more greatly than industrials.

Theoretical and empirical evidence produced to date does not support this hypothesis. Bowie (1982) showed that the impact of depreciation was likely to be far greater for offices and industrials than for retail property, but ranks industrials ahead of offices in this respect. The respective running and *true* yield differences are 22.00% and 26.67% for offices and industrials. Salway (1986) and Fraser (1986) suggest broadly similar depreciation rates (of 3% and 2% respectively) for both offices and industrials.

There is clearly some interest in the impact of depreciation upon industrial properties. While this may be of secondary importance to the impact of depreciation on offices for the majority of investors, there is a clear distinction between the retail and business (office and industrial) sectors. Additionally, it is useful to examine comparative results where possible. For these reasons, this research measures depreciation for samples of both offices (see Chapter 6) and industrials.

The selected industrial database is described in Section 5 of Chapter 5. It comprises information concerning the rental value, age and quality of 125 buildings on an industrial estate west of London.

The analyses to be carried out are:

   i   a cross-section rent analysis;
   ii a longitudinal rent analysis; and
  iii an occupier survey.

The purposes of the industrial research are both for comparison against the findings for offices described in Chapter 6 and specific to this sample. The comparative studies are:

   i   an examination of the relationship of age and depreciation to produce a general statement about depreciation rates;
   ii a measurement of the relative impact of curable and incurable depreciation; and
  iii an examination of the relationship of property factors and depreciation to compare the explanatory power of age and quality as independent variables.

The specific purposes of this analysis are:

   i   to draw conclusions concerning those building qualities which impact most upon the depreciation of industrial buildings; and
   ii to use the considerably fuller longitudinal data to generalise about the rate of depreciation of property over time, specifically the last 25-30 years. Has the pace of depreciation quickened?

The rental data collected for the purposes of the industrial study are flawed by structural shifts in the market for industrial property in the early 1980's which makes estimates of depreciation rates – the dependent variable – subject to obfuscation.

Prior to the 1980's, business space in the UK could uncontroversially be split between traditional office and industrial uses. This distinction was quite quickly eroded in the early 1980's as so-called *high-technology* developments became popular. While definitions of this development type are elusive (for a selection of attempts, see Hillier Parker, 1987, Hall and Markusen, 1985, and Waldy, 1986) the common perception is of a less clear distinction between industrial and office space, created primarily by the research and development functions of electronics-based industries.

Henneberry (1984) and Hillier Parker (1988) allow the growth of this phenomenon to be dated with some clarity. Hillier Parker's Hi-Tech Rent Index has a datum of 1984. Writing in 1983, Henneberry refers to recent "wide coverage in the property press" of "the development of science parks, high-technology industrial estates and other similar schemes". The first half of the 1980's clearly witnessed a major shift in the use of business space.

Henneberry (1984) undertook a survey of such developments and attempted a classification based on the nature of occupiers, and also estimated the division of their use of space between offices, laboratories, manufacturing/production and storage. He found that both science park and hi-tech scheme occupiers use a markedly higher proportion of their floorspace for office use than do occupiers of conventional industrial estates. Hi-tech scheme occupiers used 51% of space as offices; conventional estate occupiers used 14% in this way.

Evans and Plumb (1984) found that "knowledge-based industries" which would dominate occupation of hi-tech space had very great requirements for flexibility of use, necessitating a higher standard of building quality.

It is clear that the reduced distinction between office and manufacturing space which prompted enquiry in the early 1980's led to problems of classification and to an increase in the average quality and value of what previously would have been designated industrial buildings. Hence an estimation of depreciation on an industrial estate affected by this shift will be coloured by the divergence of values created by the differences in the quality, flexibility and use of industrial space which in turn resulted from structural shifts in the market for occupation of business space. The result for the purposes of this study is somewhat lesser reliability of depreciation estimates against comparable measures for the office sample analysed in Chapter 6.

Subject to these reservations, Section 2 (below) describes the cross-sectional rent analysis which is used to produce the comparative studies listed above. This also provides evidence for measuring the relative importance of different building qualities, which is further tested by an occupier survey described in Section 3. The longitudinal analysis which is presented in Section 4 allows further comparison of the relationship between age and depreciation and, further, some indication of the changing rate of building depreciation over the past twenty years. Conclusions are drawn in Section 5.

2. Cross-section rent analysis

Age against depreciation

Table 43 shows the relationship between age and smoothed ERV.

Table 43: Age against depreciation in rental value

No of properties	125
Mean age	22.97
Mean smoothed ERV (£)	5.57
Mean depreciation (£)*	1.10
Standard deviation (age)	14.51
Standard deviation (ERV £)	0.77
Regression equation:	
Depreciation (£) =	0.37 + 0.20 age
Coefficient of correlation (r)	0.400
Coefficient of deter-	
mination ($\overline{R}^2$) (%)	15.32
Significance (t)	4.84

Note: *against a smoothed average rent for new buildings (age 0 and 1) of £6.67

Table 44 presents a description of rental depreciation connected with the ageing process. This shows a very rapid decrease in rental value as a new industrial building becomes second-hand. This is partially explained by the advent of *hi-tech* buildings in the early 1980's. Depreciation is then very slow. The average rate is considerably slower than the annual averages of 2% suggested by Fraser (1986) and the 3.3% over 20 years found by Salway (1986). The 40-year average rate found in this study is around 0.5% per annum; the 20-year rate is similar. This difference is at least partially explained by the relatively high site values which pertain for the subject estate, which is arguably one of the prime industrial locations in the UK. The pattern of depreciation shown in the index column is one of rapid depreciation, then very slow depreciation and gently increasing depreciation thereafter until, after year 30, differences in age become almost irrelevant in determining rent.

Property factors against ERV and total depreciation

As a next stage, depreciation in ERV was correlated with the appraised qualities of the buildings. These were office content, building quality, site cover and accessibility, lot size having been smoothed away from the rent data.

Regression analysis showed that only two of the variables were significant at the 95% level. These were building quality and accessibility/immediate environs. A two-variable model (Equation 7) was therefore tested, in which the amount of depreciation suffered by each property was calculated by reference to the shortfall of the actual rent from a prime rent for the estate as at the 1986 valuation date. The building quality and accessibility variables are expressed as shortfalls from their highest possible score of 5.

Table 44: Depreciation in ERV and age band

Age	Frequency	Mean age	Mean smoothed ERV (£)	Index	Dep'n rate pa (%)	Years
0-4	23	2.13	6.36	100		
5-9	9	6.77	5.96	93.71	2.95	2-7
10-14	9	11.56	5.86	92.14	0.33	7-12
15-19	10	17.90	5.75	90.41	0.52	12-18
20-29	24	23.50	5.53	86.95	0.62	18-24
30-39	10	32.00	5.12	80.50	0.76	24-32
40	39	40.00	5.05	79.40	0.14	32-40

Mean annual depreciation rate: 0.52%

Equation 7: Depreciation and property factors

Depreciation in ERV $= 0.183 + 0.289a1 + 0.119 a2$

where	a1	$= 5$ - building quality score, and $t = 7.95$
	a2	$= 5$ - accessibility score, and $t = 3.55$

$$\overline{R}^2 = 42.7\%$$

Building quality is the most important variable, which encourages a more detailed analysis of this factor as a means of comparing office and industrial samples. This is described in Section 3.

Curable and incurable depreciation

The panel of valuers was also asked to estimate the rental value of each property at the 1986 valuation date assuming it had undergone a cost-effective refurbishment in line with the definition and method described in Chapter 6. The change in scores for the property factors was also recorded. Where an improvement to the property would not have been cost-effective, neither the scores nor the rent were changed.

From these results, the degree of curable and incurable depreciation was estimated. It is interesting to note the relative impact of curable and incurable depreciation over the estate as a whole. The average total depreciation in the sample was 32.48%: curable depreciation averaged 3.15%, while incurable depreciation averaged 29.33%. Clearly incurable depreciation is by far the most important of the two types of depreciation, implying that the scope for cost-effective refurbishment is restricted on the industrial estate. This contrasts sharply with the City office research, where the split between curable and incurable depreciation was roughly equal.

Correlations between property factors and curable and incurable depreciation are similar. This indicates that multiple regression equations using these factors as independent variables would be subject to multicollinearity. The following sections attempt an analysis which will avoid this problem to some degree.

Curable depreciation

Curable depreciation refers to the shortfall in rent of a particular building that can be addressed by some form of refurbishment. Nothing can be done about accessibility and immediate environs, so this factor will have no effect on curable depreciation. The factors which are most easily changed are building quality and office content, and it is changes in these that best explain curable depreciation. In only two cases would the site cover have been changed following a cost-effective refurbishment, so this tends to be relatively unimportant and insignificant. This suggests, *a priori*, a two-variable model for explaining curable depreciation. It is shown below as Equation 8, and confirms building quality as the most important factor affecting curable depreciation.

Equation 8: Curable depreciation and property factors

Depreciation in ERV $= 0.004 + 0.237z_1 + 0.081z_2$

---

where z_1 = refurbished building quality score, and t = 12.16
        z_2 = refurbished office content score, and t = 4.35

$$\bar{R}^2 = 65.3\%$$

Incurable depreciation

Incurable depreciation refers to the rental shortfall of a building in its refurbished state from the estate prime rent. For example, following refurbishment a property may increase its building quality score from 3 to 4, its other scores may not change and its rent may increase from £4 to £5. The hypothesised explanation for the difference between the top rent on the estate and the refurbished rent of £5 is the difference between the top score possible for each property factor (5) and the scores as refurbished, including the building quality score of 4.

Office content and site cover were found to be of little importance in predicting incurable depreciation; both were statistically insignificant. Building quality and accessibility and immediate environs were found to be the important variables, as shown in Equation 9 below.

Equation 9: Incurable depreciation and property factors

Incurable depreciation in ERV $= 0.174 + 0.306z1 + 0.117z2$

where	$z1 = 5$ - refurbished building quality score, and $t = 6.72$
	$z2 = 5$ - acccessibility, and $t = 3.48$

$$\overline{R}^2 = 36.0\%$$

Since incurable depreciation is far more important than curable depreciation, and given that (i) building quality and (ii) accessibility and immediate environs are most important in explaining incurable depreciation, the conclusion can therefore be drawn that building quality and accessibility explain total building depreciation to a considerable degree, thereby confirming Equation 7.

3. A survey of occupiers

It is clear that building quality is the most important factor in predicting total, curable and incurable depreciation in ERV. This is an important finding: it means that the classification model constructed in Chapter 4 is at least largely of use in the industrial study. From this it is possible to confirm the importance of building depreciation as a cause of depreciation in rental value, and it can also be derived that an analysis of the relative importance of physical deterioration and building obsolescence factors, on the model of Chapter 6, will be meaningful.

As indicated previously, building quality scores were based very much on a general impression rather than a detailed knowledge of each individual building. It is not therefore possible from the cross-sectional analysis to draw detailed conclusions.

However, a survey of the 125 occupiers of the estate provided further supporting information regarding the importance of sub-factors within building quality. To test this, using expert advice building quality was divided into nine sub-factors; occupiers were then asked to rate how important they considered each factor to be. The response rate was 32%, providing 40 data points.

The sub-factors were rated using the following scale.

1. Not at all important
2. Of some importance
3. Of average importance
4. Very important
5. Of prime importance

By summating the scores for each sub-factor, it is possible to determine which building quality factors, in the eyes of the occupiers, are of most importance in influencing location decisions. The results are as shown in Table 45.

Table 45: Building quality sub-factors (1)

Sub-factor	Total score	Average score	Rank
State of repair/level of det'n	165	4.125	1
Level of maintenance required	158	3.950	2
Column-free space	155	3.875	3
Quantity of M & E services	145	3.625	4
Floor loading	141	3.525	5
Level of insulation	140	3.500	6
External appearance	136	3.400	7
Eaves height	127	3.175	8
Air-conditioning	39	2.325	9

If occupier preferences are accurate indicators of rents paid, then it is reasonable to assume that those building sub-factors considered of prime importance will play a large role in determining depreciation. For example, column-free space was considered to be very important. Therefore buildings with unclear floorspace will tend to have suffered high degrees of depreciation. Conversely, occupiers in general consider eaves heights to be relatively unimportant; low eaves heights should not therefore depress rents greatly.

Occupiers agreed that the state of repair/level of deterioration was the most important building sub-factor. From this one would conclude that badly deteriorated buildings let for less than buildings in good condition; and this is confirmed by the fact that older buildings let for less than new buildings. Since an old building will probably require more maintenance than a new one, the cost of running that building will be higher, therefore depressing the rent. It is consequently not surprising that the level of maintenance required was considered to be the second most important sub-factor and this reinforces the importance of state of repair and physical deterioration. It is interesting to note that the level of insulation was also considered to be reasonably important (6th). The factors taking up the 1st, 2nd and 6th places in the ranking all involved direct cost to the occupier. If occupier preferences do correlate with rental value then rents will be discounted to reflect abnormally high running costs.

The factor considered to be least important by occupiers was air-conditioning. For certain types of businesses air-conditioning is of prime importance and high rents will be paid for buildings offering this amenity. Given this fact, its importance to the other businesses is likely to be even more negligible than Table 45 suggests is the case for the whole sample.

A comparison with the findings of the City office research may now facilitate a judgement of the relative importance of building qualities for offices and industrials. In the office study, building qualities were divided into the following categories: deterioration, configuration of space, internal specification and external appearance. It is possible to group the industrial building sub-factors above into these categories and then to compare their relative importance with the results of the City research.

Some initial simplification is possible. Firstly, the provision of air-conditioning is considered unimportant by the average occupier in the industrial estate, and this sub-factor may be dropped from the analysis. Secondly, as the level of maintenance required will be so dependent on the state of repair and level of deterioration, these factors may be combined. This leaves seven sub-factors. These are then allocated to the City office categories and ranked as shown in Table 46.

Industrial occupiers arguably consider deterioration to be the most important of the four categories, and external appearance to be the least important. It is difficult to distinguish between the relative ranking of the other two factors: configuration factors occupy 2nd and 7th places whilst internal specification factors are ranked 3rd and 5th.

However, this is sufficient to make a comparison with the City office research. In the City the factors were ranked in the following order of importance in determining rental depreciation: internal specification, configuration, external appearance, and finally deterioration.

The most dramatic difference is the reversal of deterioration, from most important for industrial property to least important for City offices. This can be explained by the nature of the businesses involved. Office users are concerned with well serviced, attractive, functional work environments. The quality of the work environment is clearly less important to the average industrial occupier, who is instead more concerned that the building in which he works is in good functional condition, thus keeping maintenance costs to a minimum. This prompts several possible conclusions regarding the design of industrial and office buildings, particularly given different patterns in the ownership and occupation of these sectors.

Table 46: Building quality sub-factors (2)

Sub-factor	Category	Rank
State of repair/ level of det'n/ level of maintenance required	Deterioration	1
Column-free space	Configuration	2
Quantity of M&E services	Internal specification	3
Floor loading	Other	4
Level of insulation	Internal specification	5
External appearance	External appearance	6
Eaves heights	Configuration	7

4. Longitudinal rent analysis

A longitudinal rent analysis of the industrial data was carried out with two purposes. Firstly, as in the office study described in Chapter 6, a longitudinal analysis of rents provides information regarding depreciation rates over building life (age against depreciation) which may (with care) be directly compared with the results of a cross-section rent analysis. (For offices, the cross-section result was broadly confirmed by the longitudinal study: see Table 30.)

Secondly, given the considerably more abundant data which is available for a longitudinal analysis of the industrial sample (see below), it is possible (again, with care) to make a statement about the rate of depreciation of property over time, in order to answer the question: has the pace of deprecation quickened?

Several difficulties arise in attempting a longitudinal analysis of property rental values. These were discussed in full in Chapter 5, but some repetition is useful at this stage. Firstly, while location factors are not seen to be important in 1986, given that it is not possible to hold this factor constant over time there is some risk that there were differences in site values in the past. This would colour the rate of depreciation and reduce the quality of the data. Secondly, historic valuations are sometimes in respect of units of a different size to those currently in existence. This might happen where buildings have been divided into smaller units since the original valuation, or where a tenant previously occupying one part of a large building split into units has subsequently expanded his business and taken over an adjoining unit. This necessitates the exclusion of certain buildings from the analysis. Thirdly, because the level of deterioration, the office content and occupiers' perceptions of building quality may all have changed over the period of the valuations, no attempt is made to relate building quality to depreciation in the longitudinal analysis.

However, a longitudinal study has some advantages over a cross-section study. For example, there is no need to smooth data to take account of the influence of lot size upon rental value. Consequently the rental values used are unsmoothed.

The need to exclude from the sample any properties which have been changed in size, refurbished or redeveloped over the analysis period means that the sample is not as large as that used in the cross-sectional study. However, because the rate of redevelopment and refurbishment is much lower for industrial property than for City offices this is not as great a problem as it was for the City research. Data is therefore more abundant.

Valuation data, specifically estimated rental values, are available at July 1966, 1972, 1976, 1979, 1982, 1984 and 1986. The further back the analysis is taken, the fewer the number of the original 125 properties which remain, due to refurbishment and so on. To cover the full period of 1966 to 1986, useful data is available on 68 properties.

Age against depreciation

This data is now used to assess the relationship between depreciation and age. Table 47 below summarises the results. Figure 10 illustrates this relationship.

Table 47 is of reduced value, as it captures depreciation roughly between ages 20 and 40 only, and because the change in the industrial market after the period 1979 to 1986 colours that part of the data. Some restricted analysis is, however, possible.

Firstly, it is useful to consider the negative depreciation rate between 1976 and 1979. As the sample of 68 properties moves through time to a new valuation, it becomes older and less valuable. The average ERV expressed as a percentage of the prime ERV would therefore be expected to fall at every valuation to confirm a positive correlation between age and depreciation in ERV. This is indeed the case, with the exception of the period 1976 to 1979 when the prime ERV rose considerably (at around 17% per annum), but the gap closed as a result of the average ERV of the sample increasing at the higher rate of 18% per annum. Negative depreciation thus appears to have occurred. In Chapter 5, Section 3, the cyclical nature of property was suggested as a cause of unclear depreciation patterns. These may result from the closing of gaps between poor and first class properties during and in anticipation of a rising market, and Table 47 appears to be evidence of this phenomenon.

Table 47: Longitudinal analysis, 1966 - 1986

Year	Mean sample age (years)	Prime ERV (A) (£)	Mean ERV (B) (£)	B/A (%)	Dep'n (%)	Dep'n since last valuation (%)	Dep'n pa (%)
1966	21.01	0.54	0.47	87.94	12.06		
1972	27.01	0.93	0.79	84.42	15.58	3.52	0.58
1976	31.01	1.91	1.58	82.69	17.31	1.73	0.43
1979	34.01	3.03	2.61	86.05	13.95	(3.36)	(1.13)
1982	37.01	4.30	3.31	77.00	23.00	9.05	2.93
1984	39.01	5.10	3.57	70.09	29.91	6.91	3.40
1986	41.01	6.41	4.17	65.07	34.93	5.02	2.48

Mean annual depreciation rate: 0.87%

Notes: 1. Prime ERV is defined in Table 47 as the average of the ten highest unsmoothed rental values in the complete and original database of 125 properties.
2. Mean age is mean actual age, with no cut-off point used.

Secondly, some tentative conclusions regarding the relationship of depreciation and age may be made. To assist in this a comparison of analysed depreciation rates over the 20- to 40-year age using cross-section (Table 44) and longitudinal (Table 47) data is shown in Table 48.

Figure 10: Depreciation over time (a longitudinal analysis)

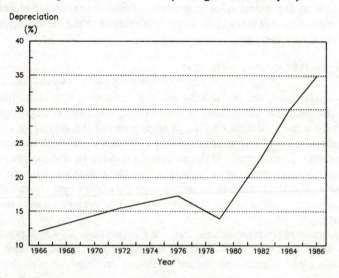

Table 48: Depreciation rate and age: comparison of cross-section and longitudinal results

Cross-section		Longitudinal	
Mean Age	Mean rent/ prime rent	Age	Mean rent/ prime rent
23.50	86.95	21.01	87.94
32.00	80.50	31.01	82.69
40.00	79.40	41.01	65.07

The clearest conclusion from this table is the absolute level of depreciation over the first 20 years of life. Salway (1986) found industrial rental values for 20-year-old buildings to be, on average, 52% of prime new value. This research is clear that on the subject estate the appropriate figure is around 87/88%. This suggests that site values constitute a very high percentage of total property value on this estate, and/or that depreciation has been abnormally slow.

Table 48 also shows a discrepancy at age 40. This is a direct and simple function of differences in the mean smoothed ERV (£5.05) in the cross-section analysis summarised in Table 41 and the mean unsmoothed ERV of the sample of 68 (£4.17) in the longitudinal analysis. The effect of smoothing is particularly great in 1986 as a result of the market change referred to in Section 1, exaggerating this discrepancy at age 40, but causing the similarity of conclusion at age

20 to be somewhat misleading. While it should thus be taken only as a guide to depreciation levels at age 20, Table 48 remains an indicator of depreciation levels which are considerably less than those suggested in the CALUS report.

Depreciation rates over time

The data presented in Table 47 are of a static sample of 68 buildings. As the sample is moved through time, changes in rates of depreciation can be attributed either to the changing age of the sample or to the changing pace of depreciation in the population from which the sample is taken. Consequently, if the evidence provided by this sample were to support an increasing depreciation rate, this may mean that buildings such as this depreciate at an increasing rate as they age; alternatively, it may mean that the pace of depreciation has accelerated over recent years.

Certain of the conclusions drawn in Chapters 6 and 7 are dependent upon an assumption of constant economic conditions, so that the reliability of conclusions regarding future performance will depend upon, for example, similar rates of technological change or building decay over the future as was experienced in the past (longitudinal) or present (cross-section) market. In order to advise decision-making, it would, therefore, be useful to examine whether the pace of depreciation has been increasing. Analysts may then interpret this information to model the future.

It would be possible to examine this issue by constructing consistent data sets of buildings of all ages at a base year, and moving each sample through different time periods. Conclusions might then be drawn concerning the pace of depreciation over different time periods. The data requirements of such an analysis are potentially massive, but this industrial data presents a limited opportunity. A data set of 68 properties which can be moved through 1966 to 1986 has already been described. It is possible to construct a second data set of 81 properties not refurbished or built after 1972 and to move that data set through the period 1972 to 1986. Similarly, data sets of 91, 95 and 104 properties can be moved through the periods 1976 to 1986, 1979 to 1986 and 1982 to 1986 respectively. All five data sets will include properties which are new, of maximum (40-year) age and intervening ages at the base year. Consequently, differences in average annual depreciation rates should be explained largely by differences in the pace of depreciation over the analysis periods rather than by differences in the age profiles of the five samples, as long as there is consistency of age profiles. Table 49 below compares means and standard deviation of all five samples at 1986, and broadly confirms that consistency exists between these samples.

Table 49: Age profiles, longitudinal data sets

Data set	Number	Mean age at 1986	Standard deviation of age at 1986
1966-86	68	33.17	8.24
1972-86	81	32.14	8.66
1976-86	91	30.49	9.83
1979-86	95	30.89	9.80
1982-86	104	29.99	10.96

Table 50 summarises depreciation patterns over the five periods covered by these data sets of broadly similar industrial property samples.

Table 50: Longitudinal analysis of depreciation (%), 5 data sets

Sample	Dep'n at end year	Dep'n at start year	Total dep'n over period	Dep'n rate per annum
1966-86	34.93	12.06	22.87	1.03
1972-86	35.37	14.99	20.28	1.33
1976-86	34.71	16.20	18.51	1.71
1979-86	34.57	12.75	21.82	2.86
1982-86	33.62	21.94	11.68	2.80

Note: all depreciation rates and values are sample means.

Two clear conclusions can initially be drawn from Table 50. Firstly, it would appear that the two longitudinal studies of offices and industrials show strikingly different depreciation rates over recent years. In the office research, the longitudinal study found average depreciation rates since 1980 to be 0.78% per annum (see Chapter 6, Section 3); depreciation in the industrial sample since 1979 has, in contrast, been 2.86% per annum. It would appear that the industrial property sample has recently depreciated at a faster rate than the City offices sample.

Secondly, the results show that depreciation rates have been increasing over the analysis period, and (given that depreciation over the later years is common to all samples, thereby increasing the average depreciation rate of the sample above that suffered in the early years) rates in the past few years have been significantly higher than in the 1960's and early 1970's. This is most clearly illustrated by comparing depreciation rates over 1972 to 1976 and 1982 to 1986. This is attempted in Table 51 which is derived partly from Table 47 and additionally utilises a part of the 1982-1986 data set referred to in Tables 48 and 49.

Table 51 shows a depreciation rate over the period 1982 to 1986 of nearly 7 times the rate of 1972 to 1976 for a sample which is similar in all important respects, including age. The explanation of differing depreciation rates is therefore to do with differences in the periods under examination and not differences in sample ages.

A very strong reservation must be set against both of these conclusions. As stated in Section 1, in the years immediately prior to 1986 there had been a radical change in the industrial property market, which forced prime rental levels through previous barriers and generally increased the range of possible rental values for industrial buildings. This increases apparent depreciation rates over the latter years of the analysis period, with considerably greater impact upon the annual depreciation rates of 1979-1986 and 1982-1986. Table 51 must therefore be viewed in the light of this problem.

Table 51: Accelerating depreciation, 1972-6 and 1982-6

Data set	Base year	Mean (1) (years)	Mean (2) (%)	Mean (3) (%)	Mean dep'n (%)	Mean dep'n pa (%)
1972-76	1972	27.01	84.42	82.69	1.73	0.43
1982-86	1982	27.43	78.06	66.38	11.68	2.92

Notes: (1) Mean sample age at base year
(2) Mean ERV/Prime ERV at base year
(3) Mean ERV/Prime ERV at base year + 4

Although this problem is not confined to the longitudinal analysis, its effect is much greater than in the cross-section. This is an indirect result of the size smoothing process. The average size of the 125 buildings is around 15,500 square feet. Yet the 10 most valuable buildings in terms of unsmoothed 1986 ERV are of an average size of 2,400 square feet, with eight of these entering the data for the first time at the 1986 valuation, and the others having been refurbished in 1982 and 1984.

Site smoothing applied to the cross-section thus greatly reduces the spread of the data at 1986, and erases the effect of the newer and smaller buildings. Given the magnitude of the size smoothing factor, the effect is to pull the smoothed ERV of the older larger buildings above the mean of the small new buildings, reducing the apparent mean depreciation of the cross-section sample at 1986 and somewhat cancelling the effect of the introduction into the market of hi-tech properties.

In Table 51 the ratio of mean ERV to prime ERV at the base years of 1972 and 1982 is compared with the same ratio at 1976 and 1986. As the industrial property market had been affected materially by the appearance of high-tech properties in the early 1980s, the last ratio (mean ERV to prime ERV at 1986) is most materially affected. Given that these are unsmoothed values, this ratio is inevitably considerably lower in value, as prime ERV has begun to stretch away from the mean value. This also affects Table 50, which analyses unsmoothed values.

The longitudinal analysis must be critically reviewed in this light. The cross-sectional analysis is also affected, but to a lesser degree as a result of the smoothing process. The problem does not apply to the office research described in Chapter 6. Hence while it appears to be true that industrial buildings have been depreciating more rapidly than office buildings, and also that the rate of depreciation has been accelerating in recent years, there is some question about the degree to which these conclusions may be uncritically accepted.

5. Conclusions and comparisons

In Section 1 of this chapter it was stated that the industrial research would produce information which would be used for comparison against the findings for offices described in Chapter 6; and, additionally, it would produce some conclusions which are specific to this industrial study. The major specific result concerns the accelerating pace of depreciation and is discussed immediately above. This section therefore concentrates upon comparative results.

Firstly, a comparison of the relative depreciation rates of offices and industrials may be drawn by examining the results of the tests of age against depreciation. The two estimates of mean annual depreciation rate for industrials are 0.52% per annum from the cross-section study (Table 44) and 0.87% per annum from the longitudinal study (Table 47). These cover 40-year periods. Over the first 20 years, these figures are roughly 0.5% and 0.6% respectively. This compares with rates of around 0.75% (cross-section) over a 35-year life for offices; the respective 20-year figure is around 0.4% per annum. (There was no longitudinal study of offices covering this period.) A straightforward conclusion is that depreciation rates have been broadly similar.

These results may be compared with the findings of the CALUS report. The result of such a comparison is to suggest much lower rates of depreciation for both these office and industrial samples than the CALUS average of around 3% per annum for both data sets. This may be the result of relatively high site values for both City offices and

London region industrials. Alternatively, it may suggest that depreciation is less of a problem than the CALUS research, based on hypothetical buildings, had concluded was the case. A combination of these causes is also a possible explanation for the divergence of results.

It was stated in Section 4 that the longitudinal study of industrials showed a depreciation rate over the period 1979 to 1986 of 2.86%, which compares with a rate of 0.78% over a similar period for City offices. This might suggest a massive divergence over recent years, but the problems inherent in this analysis largely invalidate such a conclusion. Instead it would seem reasonable to concentrate on longer term averages and to remember that the rapid change in industrial building standards in the early 1980's has particularly affected the results of the longitudinal study of industrials.

Secondly, the relative importance of curable and incurable depreciation is markedly different for offices (49% and 51% respectively) than for industrials (10% and 90% respectively). The scope for cost-effective refurbishment of industrials is clearly much less than for offices.

Thirdly, while property factors are clearly superior to age as an explanation of depreciation for both offices and industrials, the relative importance of building quality types is different. Deterioration is most important for industrials, and least important for offices. Differences in the formal and perceived obligations of landlords and tenants between the two types may be instrumental in explaining this reversal, which considerably reduces the relative importance of building obsolescence in the industrial property market, while it remains clearly superior as an explanation of office depreciation.

Chapter 8

A depreciation-sensitive model for the analysis of property investments

1. Introduction

Chapter 2 of this book examines the way in which explicit or cash flow models may be used in the analysis of property investments. It discusses the various formats which have been developed and goes into detail regarding the variables which have to be accounted for. A basic model is presented in Section 3 of that chapter for illustration purposes and to form the basis of a depreciation-sensitive model. This chapter develops a depreciation-sensitive model, which is of some value not primarily *per se* but as a means of exploring the impact of depreciation in the latter sections.

The features of the basic model are summarised as follows. A finite holding period is utilised and a 15-year analysis period chosen. The model is explicit regarding rental growth, risk premium, costs of management and resale yield. The basis of analysis is NPV and IRR and a standard risk-free opportunity cost yield is chosen as the benchmark. The model is framed in nominal terms (although it is recognised that analysis in real terms will be increasingly necessary).

The introduction of building depreciation into this framework raises several questions. Should depreciation be dealt with deterministically as a third independent variable, worthy of exploration alongside the risk premium and forecasts of rental and capital growth? Should depreciation be dealt with as a stochastic variable which impacts solely upon the risk premium? Are both approaches necessary?

In Chapter 3, a further question arose. Sykes (1984b) proposed a model in which the necessary expenditure on a building was used as a proxy for building depreciation. Is forecast expenditure alternatively the best means of modelling depreciation in a depreciation-sensitive model?

In Chapters 6 and 7, the relative importance of curable and incurable depreciation was measured. It was shown that for City offices the two factors were of roughly equal importance. For the industrials sample, incurable depreciation was much more important. The remaining question is, therefore, whether an allowance for required expenditure to address *curable* depreciation is an effective input into a depreciation-sensitive model. These questions are addressed below.

A third variable?

In Chapter 2, Section 4 develops a simple equation for the explicit analysis of property investments prior to a consideration of depreciation. That equation is:

$$k = \text{RFR} + r - g$$

where k = the initial yield for a fully let property;
   RFR = the risk-free inflation-prone opportunity cost rate;
   r = the risk premium; and
   g = income growth.

This exposes r and g as the two variables which require exploration by property investment analysts. The growing interest in depreciation raised the possibility that it be considered as a third variable which fundamentally determines the attractiveness of a property investment and should therefore be dealt with explicitly in an analytical model.

In the equation, given that depreciation has been shown to be a variable which impacts upon rental value and therefore rental growth, it is clear that g is a net of depreciation rate. Redefining g as expected average rental growth in continually new buildings (as measured by most indices, including the Investors Chronicle Hillier Parker Rent Index), the equation should therefore be amended to:

$$k = \text{RFR} + r - (g - d) \text{ or } k = \text{RFR} + r - g + d$$

In the equation this sets out the three variables r, g and d for analysis. As it is clear that depreciation or (more correctly) deterioration and obsolescence impacts upon the return from property investments (see Chapter 3), in the context of an explicit model it should arguably be dealt with explicitly.

At this point it is useful to examine some continuing definitional problems. In Chapter 4, depreciation and obsolescence were distinguished as effect and cause. Hence, it would appear incorrect to talk of depreciation as a cause of a loss of investment return; by definition, it is a loss in value, and these are the same thing. However, there is a distinction to be drawn, because depreciation has been defined as a loss in the real existing use value of a property investment. It may be that a property suffering depreciation will not suffer a loss of return or value because, for example, its site value is dominant. Additionally it is expedient to continue to use the term depreciation as a blanket term to cover both deterioration and obsolescence, which are both *causes* of a loss in value.

Certain technical issues remain to be dealt with. Pursuing the questions raised in Chapter 2 and repeated above, it is necessary to decide whether depreciation should be input as a separate variable or whether g and d may be combined to produce a net of depreciation rental growth rate. It is also necessary to consider the impact of depreciation upon the risk of property investment. For example, reference was made in Chapter 6 to the flexibility of buildings as a risk minimiser. This recognises that certain buildings are more at risk of depreciation (and especially obsolescence) than others. Given that depreciation is a stochastic variable which cannot be predicted with confidence, its introduction as a new third variable must carry with it the need to recognise that it impacts upon property risk (the chance that return will not be as expected). This can be dealt with in either of two ways: deterministically, by adjusting the target rate or income flow (these risk adjustment techniques are described in Chapter 2); or probabilistically by constructing a distribution of possible outcomes. Finally, the treatment of forecast required expenditure must be considered. It is possible to cope with *curable* depreciation in this way.

These issues are considered in Section 2 below. Before this is attempted, existing depreciation-specific models are briefly reviewed, and the preferred framework for the final model is introduced.

Existing models

Explicit cash flow models have been developed to date as a response to post-1960 conditions of inflation and a post-1974 realisation of the danger that traditional valuation practices based on simplistic comparison produce a self-perpetuating market. In the refinement of the models, much work has concentrated upon (a) projections of future rental value and (b) the appropriate target rate, as noted above.

Rental growth is widely allowed for by assuming a constant rate of increase over a holding period. This can be assumed to ignore depreciation in rental value. In fact depreciation has generally been excluded from the debate referred to above with the exception of papers in a special issue of *Journal of Valuation* (5:2, 1987) in which three papers present depreciation-explicit cash flow models (Salway, 1987, Miles, 1987, and Harker, 1987) and a paper by Sykes (1984b) which adopts a different approach by using required expenditure as a proxy for depreciation.

The latter paper has already been criticised in this book for its lack of recognition of the importance of incurable depreciation. Given that Chapter 6 found office depreciation to be split roughly equally between curable and incurable depreciation, and that Chapter 7 found the relative weight of incurable depreciation to be as high as 90% for industrials, Sykes' model can be rejected as a means of explicitly addressing depreciation in property investment analysis.

Harker, Miles and Salway adopt similar explicit cash flow models but deal with depreciation in slightly different ways. Miles uses a model very similar to that illustrated in Chapter 2, but uses rates of rental growth which decline from current implied rates to account for depreciation. Given that implied rates are necessarily *net* of depreciation, this is problematic. Harker explicitly raises this problem and deals with it by grossing-up the implied growth rate which is net of an assumed depreciation rate and using that grossed-up value as the dependent variable in an analysis of a warehouse investment. This is sound, but the focus on rental growth as the dependent variable is not helpful for the purposes of this work.

Salway's suggested solution (Salway, 1986 and 1987) involves the projection of income net of depreciation over a standard lease period with reversions to a probability-weighted value which takes into account all of (i) residual site value (ii) residual value for refurbishment and (iii) investment value if re-let unimproved. This technique has two main drawbacks. Firstly, the estimation of residual value for refurbishment is highly complex, and it is unrealistic to expect that it can be done with a reasonable degree of accuracy. There are many refurbishment alternatives in most cases, implying different costs, different improved values and therefore different residual values. Which should be used? Secondly, the combination of three alternative residual values into a single weighted reversion is unrealistic and may double-count risk by combining a modified certainty equivalent approach with a risk-adjusted discount rate. Assuming that such a model will certainly utilise a risk-adjusted discount rate, the cash flow projection should be the most likely or expected income. If site value exceeds building value, any typical investor will (as long as he is able to) demolish the building and thereby exploit site value. Site value should then be input into the model, which should automatically select the highest reversion. Any other approach would seem to be an underestimate to allow for risk, which should already be dealt with by the risk-adjusted target rate.

The preferred framework

All approaches may be criticised: no model will be satisfactory to all. The model developed in Section 3 of this chapter is suggested with confidence if only because it draws on the best features on the work briefly described above, within the framework already established in Chapter 2. It treats depreciation as a true *third variable*, whose impact on the input variables is dealt with immediately below in Section 2.

2. The impact of depreciation

From Section 1 above it is clear that a depreciation-sensitive model has to cope with the possible impact of depreciation on four input variables. These are: rent, resale yield, expenditure and the risk premium. In this section it is established exactly how this impact should be dealt with and estimated.

Indices of rental value growth are typically gross of depreciation. Given that extrapolation often influences forecasts, estimates of rental growth are also likely to be gross of depreciation. In order to construct a depreciation-explicit decision model it is therefore necessary to overlay the rent forecast with estimates of depreciation.

Forecasts of average depreciation

Based on the work described in Chapters 6 and 7, cross-section analysis naturally suggests itself as a means of estimating rent depreciation as a building ages. It would be preferable to predict depreciation by using building quality (see Chapter 6); but this would necessitate prediction of *future* building quality. Given that obsolescence factors are of overwhelming importance, and that obsolescence cannot be predicted, this would be very dangerous, and the main products of Chapter 6 are an *explanation* of depreciation and an indication of the importance of building flexibility. Age, however can be predicted with certainty, and some estimate of the reaction of rent to age (as a proxy for building quality) can be made.

A 15-year holding period is used in the decision model described in Section 3 below. Assuming 5-yearly rent reviews, this necessitates the estimation of rental value at review 1 in 5 years' time, rental value at review 2 in 10 years' time, rental value at review 3 (end of holding period) in 15 years' time and of the resale yield, for the purpose of estimating resale price. These can all be estimated by cross-section analysis, relating age to ERV and yield.

A forecast of depreciation might also be attempted by building a regression equation which combines age and building qualities. Such an equation would be expected to produce a high coefficient of determination. This has not been pursued in this chapter for the reasons stated above. It is very difficult to predict obsolescence qualities. Nonetheless, this is an approach which suggests itself for further exploration. It may be possible to predict deterioration with some confidence; age can be predicted with certainty; and a flexibility measure may proxy a forecast of obsolescence.

A cross-section analysis produces estimates of rental value and yield for buildings of different ages at the same point in time. This abstracts projections away from forecast rent receipts, because rental growth is isolated as a separate – gross of depreciation – input. With an adequate sample it is possible to assess the average rental value for similar buildings of a different age. For the purposes of the preferred decision model, estimates of the rental value of buildings comparable to the subject but 5, 10 and 15 years older are required. Similarly, an estimate of the resale capitalisation rate will be possible by finding the average yield on similar, but 15 years older, buildings. Note, however, the likely reduced availability of consistent yield data: see Chapters 5, 6 and 7.

Adjustments for building flexibility

An extensive cross-section analysis will produce estimates of *average* rates of depreciation in rental value and yield for a sample of buildings over a 15-year holding period by relating depreciation to age. This ignores the major hypothesis of this research, which is to the effect that a model which classifies the causes of depreciation will provide an explanation of depreciation which is superior to age alone. This hypothesis is proven in Chapters 6 and 7. It is now necessary to incorporate these findings in respect of *causes* of depreciation into the decision model. The model developed here is primarily guided by the office findings.

It is concluded in Chapter 4 that the precise impact of building obsolescence (a change in utility not related to the passage of time) is by its very nature impossible to predict. Given that it has been established that building obsolescence is much more important than building deterioration as a cause of depreciation, the conclusion has to be drawn that building depreciation is extremely difficult to anticipate. For any particular building, therefore, it is the building's likely resistance to potential sources of depreciation which is of fundamental importance. A decision model must be capable of reflecting a building's flexibility, and hence its resistance to depreciation. The consequence of this reasoning is that flexibility has to be measured. This may be achieved in two stages. Firstly, those factors which contribute to flexibility must be identified and measured; secondly, they must be weighted according to their relative importance. Chapters 6 and 7 provide a basis for each of these stages. They will certainly differ between offices and industrials: for the remainder of this chapter, it is the office work in Chapter 6 which is used for model development.

The appraisals carried out by a panel of City office valuers/agents reported in Chapters 5 and 6 and expanded by a survey of City office occupiers reported in Chapter 6 established four major causes of depreciation. These were as follows.

1. Configuration, including layout and floor-to-ceiling height as sub-factors, was noted as a wholly incurable building element. Hence flexibility should not be measured by the degree to which this can be cured, but by its quality.

2. Internal specification includes services and internal fittings and finishes. Flexibility in these factors will relate to the degree to which they may be altered.

3. External appearance includes the exterior of the building and the entrance hall. Flexibility in these factors is again directly related to the extent to which they may be altered.

4. Physical deterioration is partially remediable. To what extent may anticipated deterioration be corrected?

(Note that factors 2, 3, and 4 are related, as flexibility in these respects is derived directly from the *curable* element of depreciation which must be measured by both feasibility (to what extent is it *possible* to correct problems?) and viability (to what extent is it *profitable* to correct problems?).)

Breaking these four factors down into sub-factors produces a list of seven: floor layout, floor-to-ceiling height, services, internal finishes and fittings, entrance hall, external appearance and building deterioration. The relative unimportance of the latter suggests no further subdivision. The relative weighting of each is guided by the hierarchial analysis described in Chapter 6. This identified configuration, internal specification and external appearance as being more important than physical deterioration; and it also suggested that the sub-factors of floor layout, services and entrance hall were roughly twice as important as floor-to-ceiling height, internal fittings and external appearance respectively. A building flexibility model using simple weightings based on these findings is developed below. The listed factors are scored on a scale of 1 (poor) to 5 (good). The result is a total weighted score on a scale of 1 (low flexibility) to 5 (high flexibility). This is then expressed on a reduced scale where 0 to 1.67 is low flexibility, 1.68 to 3.33 is medium flexibility and 3.34 to 5 is high flexibility. An example will illustrate this process.

Step	Question	Score	Weighting
1	Is the floor layout capable of flexible use?	4	2
2	Is the floor-to-ceiling height generous?	4	1
3	Can the services be easily upgraded?	4	2
4	Are the interior fittings easily changed?	4	1
5	Are the entrance hall and common areas capable of improvement?	3	2
6	Is the external appearance capable of cost-effective alteration?	2	1
7	Is potential building deterioration likely to be curable?	4	1

Weighted average score = 36/10 = 3.60
Flexibility = high

In the decision model, therefore, three categories of building are employed to reflect flexibility. They are described as low flexibility, average flexibility and high flexibility. This allows knowledge of building quality to be incorporated as an input into a decision model. Average depreciation rates in rent and yield based on cross-section analysis of the subject market are input by the user. Adjustments for depreciation rates for low and high flexibility buildings are then made as an overlay on this average rate, and will be based in this chapter on the empirical evidence provided in Chapter 6.

It is important to recognise that the calculations of depreciation rates for low and high flexibility buildings are applicable to City offices only, and only then if it is accepted as likely that the past market behaviour which has been analysed to form the basis of the model will be continued into the future. Relative rates of depreciation for high and low flexibility buildings will presumably be different in other markets, and market-specific cross-section analysis will be necessary to produce appropriate values. Re-analysis of the City office market will also be necessary on a regular basis. Also, following from comments made in Chapter 6, a more simple or pragmatic two-variable measure of flexibility may be utilised. This might use steps 1 and 3 only to produce a weighted average score of 4 (high flexibility).

Inputs

Rent

The rental depreciation rates for low, average and high flexibility buildings were calculated as follows. Firstly, average rental depreciation rates over each review were calculated. These are derived from Table 25 in Chapter 6. Assuming a normal distribution of depreciation rates for all buildings in each review sample, it is possible to draw conclusions regarding possible variations from the average. For example, this assumption would lead to the conclusion that depreciation between the average rate and one standard deviation lower will be suffered by (on average) 34.13% of the sample.

This analysis can be extended as follows. Depreciation in excess of the mean plus one standard deviation will be suffered by 15.87% of the sample. Depreciation of between the mean and the mean plus one standard deviation will be suffered by 34.13% of the sample. Depreciation of between the mean and the mean less one standard deviation will be suffered by 34.13% of the sample. Depreciation of less than the mean less one standard deviation will be suffered by 15.87% of the sample. This type of analysis can be used to assess depreciation rates for any portion of a sample. For example, it is possible to split the distribution into three equal areas and to assign mid-points for each, thereby providing average depreciation rates for low, average and high flexibility buildings.

While such an analysis is extremely useful in data description it is dependent upon the distribution being normal. Before proceeding, this needs to be established in the case of the City office data. Rental depreciation rates were measured by grouping data into age ranges (as in Table 25). Further analyses of these data produce the following results (Table 52).

Pearson's measure of skewness (Neter, Wasserman and Whitmore, 1982) shows distributions to be positively skewed, that is to high depreciation, although for age 5-9 the distribution is near normal.

Table 53 shows the result of a check on this using slightly different groupings of data clustered around the rent review points at years 5, 10 and 15.

Table 52: Distribution of rental values (1)

Age	Frequency	Average smoothed ERV (£)	Standard deviation (£)	Skewness
5-9	31	33.12	4.18	0.05
10-14	19	32.16	3.65	0.62
15-19	10	31.22	5.55	1.05

Table 53: Distributions of rental values (2)

Age	Frequency	Average smoothed ERV (£)	Standard deviation (£)	Skewness
4-6	26	32.51	3.97	0.79
9-11	21	33.20	4.15	-0.14
13-17	10	30.92	5.16	0.64

Table 53 broadly confirms the results shown in Table 52. Skewness is generally positive. Although the age 9-11 value is slightly negative, it is close to zero, indicating a roughly normal distribution.

Given that age and depreciation are positively correlated, a skewed age distribution would reduce the general implication of Table 52. However, the age distributions for all six samples shown in Tables 52 and 53 are roughly normal. It can therefore be concluded from the skewness measures shown in Tables 52 and 53 that the City office sample shows a general skewness towards high depreciation over each band. This is to be expected. To illustrate, the average rental value for properties aged 0 to 4 years is £34.76. The average rent for properties aged 4 to 6 years is £33.32. The lowest smoothed rent in this sample is £25.90. The potential for skewness to high depreciation is clear from these figures.

Calculations of rental depreciation rates for City office buildings of high and low flexibility should therefore take account of general positive skewness (that is, biased towards high depreciation). The value of standard deviation as an interpretative measure is thereby reduced. The level of skewness is none the less sufficiently small to encourage its retention if only for illustrative purposes or for reasons of pragmatism. Consequently, the assumption of a normal distribution was retained, but the shape of the distributions was adjusted by removing outliers from the distribution and the remaining skewness was taken into account by adjusting the values of mid-points of the upper and lower thirds of the distribution. This process is described fully in Baum (1989a).

Resulting values are as shown as in Table 54.

Table 54: Adjusted rental values and age bands

Age band	Lower mid-point (%)	Central mid-point (%)	Upper mid-point (%)
5-9	90.00	95.00	97.50
10-14	80.00	90.00	95.00
15-19	75.00	87.50	93.75

Adjustment of these relationships based on expectations will be necessary for applications of the model. Albeit based on factual evidence, the above estimates are for illustration only, and refer specifically to the central City office market at mid-1986. They represent an attempt to produce realistic and pragmatic inputs into the decision model, which is utilised later in this chapter.

Yield

For yields, the above process was repeated. Table 55, derived from Table 38, shows the results for yields at years 15-19 (an approximation to the end of the holding period). Two outliers have been removed to produce a closer approximation to normality. The standard deviation is 0.34%. The adjustment reflects the fact that the actual distribution is skewed slightly towards higher yields (high depreciation).

Expenditure

It has been assumed to date that depreciation is revealed as a shortfall in rental value and/or as an excess of all risks yield against prime or best rents or yields. In Chapter 5 it was recognised that depreciation may, in addition, be disguised by expenditure upon a building. While the research method chosen dictated abstracting away from the need for and effect of expenditure, a decision model need not ignore it.

Some commentators have gone further by developing appraisal models which use regular refurbishment expenditure as the proxy for depreciation to the exclusion of yield or rental value changes: see for example, Sykes (1984b). Salway (1986) presents a model which incorporates a judgement of refurbishment expenditure at the end of the holding period in addition to modelling rental value and yield changes.

Table 55: Yield depreciation (%): upper, middle and lower mid-points

	Mean yield - 1 SD	Mean yield	Mean yield + 1 SD
Yield at year 15-19	5.44	5.78	6.12
As % of year one yield (5.02%)	108.31	115.12	121.93
Yield depreciation	8.31	15.12	21.93
Adjusted yield depreciation	10.00	15.00	25.00

Two approaches incorporating estimates of refurbishment expenditure are therefore possible. One hypothesises that regular refurbishment expenditure will maintain the rental value and yield at constant real levels. This approach is over-simplistic, failing as it does to cope with incurable depreciation. The second approach combines rising yields, falling real rental values and the need for expenditure. This is much more realistic and forms the basis of the preferred decision model.

However, there are practical limitations on such an approach. Firstly, refurbishment expenditure deals with that element of depreciation which is curable: improvement of internal finishes, of services, of entrance halls and external appearance, and repair of physical deterioration where that is both economic and possible. Much of this responsibility falls upon the shoulders of the tenant under the terms of a full repairing and insuring lease, and will be dealt with by the tenant on a regular basis or when he vacates and is faced with a dilapidations claim. To deduct expenses from the landlord's projected cash flow may therefore be largely unrealistic. Secondly, the landlord may not be given the opportunity to refurbish. If the tenant renews his lease under the terms of the 1954 Landlord and Tenant Act Part II, the landlord will not have the right to possession and will lose control: depreciation will then be evidenced wholly by falling real rents and rising yields. Thirdly, the holding period specified for any standard decision model (15 years in this case) will not necessarily coincide with a lease end or break. Access for refurbishment will be obtained only through negotiation with the tenant. Finally, as already stated, refurbishment expenditure is a stochastic variable with consequences for both yield and rent. If refurbishment is allowed for, how can the standard of refurbishment be envisaged? How can the consequent effect on rents and yields be estimated?

These difficulties again have to be dealt with pragmatically, and the following principles suggest themselves as guides to a solution. Firstly, given that a decision model will be used for new and old buildings let under a variety of leasing arrangements, the landlord may need to commit expenditure at any time in a 15-year holding period. The model should therefore be flexible. Secondly, expenditure is in respect of curable depreciation only. It should be hypothesised as that amount which needs to be expended by a landlord over a 15-year period to keep the building in a reasonable state, and no more. Otherwise, a nesting problem will arise and values for average rent and yield depreciation will become inappropriate to the subject property.

A likely scenario is, as suggested by Salway (1987), that the landlord may be assumed to gain access at the end of the holding period in order to refurbish. In this case, for the reasons stated above it should not be envisaged that anything other than a holding operation be carried out. The instability that would be introduced by the range of possible refurbishments would cause the model to become akin to a highly sensitive development appraisal. Equally likely is the prospect that no expenditure will be expected to be carried out by the landlord. Where, as is often the case, an appraisal is carried out at the grant of a new 25-year lease on full repairing and insuring terms, it may not be possible for the investor to gain access and the tenant may address all curable depreciation in the routine observance of his lease contract.

Two most likely scenarios therefore present themselves. These are, firstly, nil expenditure; and, secondly, a refurbishment to reinstate the building to a reasonable (average) state at the end of the holding period. The model should be designed to be flexible, but these are the likely ways in which expenditure will be accommodated.

The estimation of the likely amount of refurbishment expenditure required at the lease end cannot be based on the empirical evidence described in Chapter 6. The relative importance of curable depreciation is available as evidence, but the amount spent by landlords and tenants over a period on the subject buildings is not. For this reason, the illustrations will utilise the *no expenditure* scenario, which effectively assumes that the tenant will act exactly like the average tenant in reducing curable depreciation. Thus, when using cross-section analysis to compare the average rental value of new and 10-year old buildings, the lower value of the latter will be a function of incurable depreciation and that portion of curable depreciation which is not dealt with by the typical tenant.

Risk premium

Forecast depreciation, in the form of rental value and yield, is stochastic, and the choice of input value is from a distribution of possible values. There is a risk of the input value being incorrect, and the addition of depreciation as a new variable carries with it the need to allow for the risk it creates.

The risk premium in depreciation-implicit models may or may not include an allowance for depreciation. This depends on the extent to which it is recognised. Assuming a reasonably efficient market in the 1980's, a 2% risk premium arguably includes an element for the prospects of depreciation. In a depreciation-explicit model, the risk premium should therefore be *reduced*. The amount of the required reduction is impossible to estimate with confidence. It should, however, be recognised that certain building types are at different levels of risk. Some buildings – inflexible ones – are less able to cope with obsolescence than others. The risk premium for an inflexible building should therefore be higher than for a flexible one.

A simple set of values may be established for illustration. In a depreciation-implicit model where 2% is accepted as a typical risk premium, values of 1.25%, 1.5% and 1.75% appear reasonable for buildings of high, medium and low flexibility respectively in a depreciation-explicit model. In the model described in Section 3 below, these values are adopted. In general, given that different property market sectors will have different risks, it is the relativities but not the absolutes that need to be preserved.

3. The model

The basis of a decision model is described in Chapter 2. It is reproduced below. The example taken is of a property for sale at a price of £800 per square foot with a current ERV of £40 per square foot. The risk-free rate is 9% and a 2% risk premium is required. Rental growth of 8% per annum is projected over a 15-year holding period. Rent review fees of 7% of the new rent are deducted from the cash flow.

In current practice, the rental growth projection is likely to be gross of depreciation, based on extrapolation of a newly prime rent index such as the Investors Chronicle Hillier Parker version. Depreciation is taken into account implicitly as an uncertainty within the risk premium. This is faulty: some depreciation is certain to occur, and it is only the uncertainty regarding its quantum which should be dealt with in the risk premium.

DATA	
Price	£800
ERV	£40
Gilt redemption yield	9.00%
Risk premium	2.00%
Rent review fee	7.00%
Rental growth review 1	8.00%
Rental growth review 2	8.00%
Rental growth review 3	8.00%
Year 0 capitalisation rate	5.00%
Year 15 capitalisation rate	5.00%

PROJECTIONS	
	(£)
ERV, review 1	59
ERV, review 2	86
ERV, review 3	127
Net resale value	2,538

ANALYSIS	
Target rate (%)	11.00
NPV (£)	113
IRR (%)	12.27

CASH FLOW STATEMENT				
Year	Capital £	Income £	Outflow £	Net cash £
0	(800)			(800)
1		40		40
2		40		40
3		40		40
4		40		40
5		40	(4)	36
6		59		59
7		59		59
8		59		59
9		59		59
10		59	(6)	53
11		86		86
12		86		86
13		86		86
14		86		86
15	2,538	86	(9)	2,615

The development of a depreciation-explicit model from this basis requires the settling of several technical issues including a recognition of several complications. These include the following support mechanisms.

Support mechanisms

Two factors provide support for property value even in the context of high depreciation. These are upward-only rent reviews and site value.

Upward-only rent reviews

The preponderant use in the UK prime commercial property market of 20- or 25- year leases with 5-yearly reviews to current rental value or the current rent, whichever is higher, has important implications for a decision model which is explicit regarding depreciation. It is a fact disregarded in publications to date that this system provides an inbuilt safety net or floor to the amount of depreciation that can be suffered by an investor, and in a period of low inflation this becomes an important consideration in a purchase. The decision model does not therefore allow projected rental income to fall below the previous level of rent. Modifications to the model will, however, be necessary where lease ends occur during the holding period, thereby removing the support of the upward-only rent review. In the model demonstrated below, it is assumed that the lease end falls after the end of the holding period so that there is an inbuilt floor to the rent that may be achieved.

Site value

Similar factors apply in setting another floor at the lease end. Figure 2 (Chapter 4) shows how cleared site value net of demolition costs sets a floor for property value, because building depreciation does not impact upon site value. A model which captures rapidly declining rental value through high depreciation and low forecast rental growth for newly prime buildings, high yield increases over the holding period and a reasonably long holding period will have to recognise the possibility of projected building value falling below projected site value. If the landlord has a reasonable prospect of gaining possession at the lease end, the site value should be taken as the reversion value if it exceeds total property value at that point.

Depreciation factors and flexibility

Building quality is established in this research as a major factor which will influence the rate of depreciation. While building age may be useful as a forecast of average depreciation, adjustments will be needed to reflect building quality or, more specifically, flexibility. This will impact on three inputs. These are: rental value at future reviews; resale capitalisation rate (yield); and the risk premium.

Rental value

Cross-section analysis of a market will produce estimates of rental value in current terms for buildings of different ages, specifically for this purpose at years 0, 5, 10 and 15. These will be mean values derived from samples of buildings which are representative of a sub-market. Adjustments to these values will be based on the building's flexibility and the likely skewed distributions described in Section 2. The relationships demonstrated in Table 54 are taken as standard. Hence the central mid-point value for rent at each review is taken from a cross-section analysis; and values for high and low flexibility buildings are calculated using the relationships demonstrated in that table, so that at the first review the mid-point (high flexibility) is projected to be midway between rental values at year 0 and year 5, while the lower mid-point (low flexibility) is taken as showing double the projected depreciation for an average building. This standard pattern is also followed for rental value at years 10 and 15. The values reflect skewness to high depreciation for poor quality (low flexibility) buildings.

Yield

The same method is utilised to reflect building flexibility in resale yield, but uses the relationships described in Table 55. Yield depreciation for a low flexibility building is taken as 1.67 of the mean value. For a high flexibility building, this value is 0.67. Again, these values reflect skewness to high depreciation for low flexibility buildings.

Risk premium

No empirical evidence was produced in this research to facilitate the estimation of the risk premium for buildings of differing depreciation risk. Instead a set of arbitrary values was posited in Section 2, derived from a depreciation-implicit (or depreciation-inclusive) premium of 2% assumed to be the market standard for prime property investments (see Chapter 2). The suggested values are 1.5% for a depreciation-exclusive risk premium for an average (flexibility) building, and 1.25% and 1.75% respectively for high and low flexibility buildings. These values need to be made relative to the input risk premium. In general use, the model should recognise differing risk premiums for different market sectors, and adjustments from the base value should be made to reflect differing flexibility. Using the above basis, the relative values become the average risk premium adjusted by 1.167 and 0.833 for low and high flexibility buildings respectively.

Format

For simplicity, the model is based upon a standard 15-year holding period. The model is designed for fully let (non-reversionary) investments only, and it is specific for 5-yearly reviews. The layout of the model is in five parts, including a set of input variables and four outputs as follows: flexibility adjustments (which can be varied); projections; analysis; and a cash flow statement.

The input variables

Various alternatives present themselves for the inputting of rental depreciation as a variable in the decision model. These are:

i   rate per cent depreciation per annum over each review;
ii   estimated rental value at each review;
iii estimated rental value per square foot at each review; and
iv   estimated rental value at each review as a percentage of current rental value.

Both use of a cross-section analysis to research rental values over time and discussion with agents suggest a preference for (iii), which is therefore used in the model described below.

Data to be input into the model are as follows:

i   property reference (shown as 001, 002 etc);
ii   price of investment;
iii current estimated rental value/contract rent (these should equate);
iv   site value (estimated by comparison or, where necessary, as a percentage of price or value);
v   building flexibility on a scale of 1 to 3 denoting low flexibility (1), average flexibility (2) or high flexibility (3). (A model for estimation of this is presented in Section 2 of this chapter);
vi   the risk-free rate, possibly derived from an adjusted average of redemption yields on 15-year conventional gilts. The model is in nominal terms, so that the risk free rate is inflation-prone;
vii the risk premium, which will vary between property sectors;
viii rental growth over review period 1, review period 2 and review period 3 are forecast percentage rates of growth in prime property rental values over the first, second and third review periods respectively;
ix   estimated rental value at review 1, review 2 and review 3 are average depreciated rental values at each review in current terms, estimated from a cross-section analysis;

x   estimated resale capitalisation rate for a typical similar building albeit 15 years older;

xi   the rent review fee, expressed as a percentage of the new rent payable; and

xii   expenditure required by the landlord to keep the property in reasonable condition, and the year(s) in which it is likely to be expended.

Flexibility adjustments

Given these inputs for the typical building in the sector, the model then proceeds to make flexibility adjustments for buildings of low and high flexibility. These may be varied but for the immediate purpose are as follows.

1. Estimated rental value in current terms at each review is adjusted for high and low flexibility buildings reflecting the skewed distribution analysed in Section 2. Rent depreciation for low flexibility buildings is calculated as double the average rate input; for high flexibility buildings it is half.

2. The resale capitalisation rate is estimated as the input rate multiplied by a constant (0.667) for high flexibility buildings, and the input rate multiplied by another constant (1.667) for low flexibility buildings. The constants derive from an analysis of the City data, are relevant only to this sample and are not intended for general application.

3. The risk premium is increased by a standard amount (one-sixth) for a low flexibility building and reduced by the same amount for a high flexibility building.

Projections

From the inputs and with knowledge of the flexibility class of the building, projections made explicit within the model are as follows.

1. Depreciation in rental value over each review period, at current prices, is calculated as an annual straight line percentage rate (see Chapter 3) from the input rental data.

2. Depreciation in rental value is also expressed as an average straight-line rate over the 15-year holding period.

3. Yield depreciation is added in to produce an estimate of compound depreciation in capital value per annum. This is estimated by comparing the resale value at current prices with the current value.

4. The rent estimated to be receivable at each review is a compound function of depreciation in ERV and the input rental growth rate.
5. The projected site value at year 15 is a product of the current site value and rental growth over years 1 to 15. This is only a broad approximation, given that site value is a complex and general function of building costs, rental values, yields and other factors.
6. The projected net resale value is the estimated building value at year 15, combining the projected resale yield and ERV at that point.
7. The model selects the higher of 5 and 6 as the projected realisation value.

Analysis and cash flow statement

The analytical outputs of the model are, for the reasons suggested in Chapter 2, net present value and internal rate of return. A positive NPV and an IRR in excess of the target rate indicate that the decision should be to buy. The target rate is an additive function of the risk free rate and a risk premium. The cash flow statement projects the net expected cash flow from the investment.

Illustration

The example used in Chapter 2 and reproduced early in this section is now used in an illustration of the depreciation-explicit model. Further outputs are as follows. From a current ERV of £40, average ERV's at review 1, review 2 and review 3 of £38, £36 and £35 respectively are derived from the City office cross-section analysis. A resale capitalisation rate of 5.75% (increased from the initial 5%) is similarly derived. The risk premium is 1.5%, as derived in Section 2.

The five-part layout is reproduced below.

The results of three runs for low, medium and high flexibility buildings are as shown in Table 56.

Table 56: Results of illustration

Reference	Flexibility	NPV (£)	IRR (%)	Target rate (%)	Buy?
001	Low	(88)	9.59	10.75	No
002	Average	9	10.61	10.50	Yes
003	High	72	11.08	10.25	Yes

INPUT VARIABLES		
Property reference		002
Price	(£)	800
ERV	(£)	40
Site value	(£)	500
Building flexibility		2
Risk free rate	(%)	9.00
Risk premium	(%)	1.50
Rental growth review 1 pa	(%)	8.00
Rental growth review 2 pa	(%)	8.00
Rental growth review 3 pa	(%)	8.00
Current ERV review 1	(£)	38
Current ERV review 2	(£)	36
Current ERV review 3	(£)	35
Current capitalisation rate	(%)	5.00
Resale capitalisation rate	(%)	5.75
Rent review fee	(%)	7.00
Expenditure: amount		0
Expenditure: year		0

FLEXIBILITY ADJUSTMENTS			
Building flexibility	Low (1)	Average (2)	High(3)
Current ERV at review 1 (£)	36	38	39
Current ERV at review 2 (£)	32	36	38
Current ERV at review 3 (£)	30	35	38
Resale capitalisation rate (%)	7.00	5.75	5.25
Risk premium (%)	1.75	1.50	1.25

PROJECTIONS		
Projected ERV dep'n pa, review 1	(%)	0.98
Projected ERV dep'n pa, review 2	(%)	1.03
Projected ERV dep'n pa, review 3	(%)	0.55
Projected average SL ERV dep'n pa 1	(%)	0.79
Projected average CV dep'n pa 2	(%)	1.44
Projected ERV, review 1	(£)	56
Projected ERV, review 2	(£)	78
Projected ERV, review 3	(£)	111
Projected site value	(£)	1,586
Projected net resale	(£)	1,931
Projected realisation	(£)	1,931

Notes: 1. Straight-line estimated rental value depreciation per annum
         2. Capital value depreciation per annum

ANALYSIS	
Target rate (%)	10.50
NPV (£)	9.00
IRR (%)	10.61

CASH FLOW STATEMENT			
Year	Capital (£)	Income (£)	Outflow (£)	Net cash (£)
---	---	---	---	---
1	(800)	40		(800)
2		40		40
3		40		40
4		40		40
5		40	4	36
6		56		56
7		56		56
8		56		56
9		56		56
10		56	5	50
11		78		78
12		78		78
13		78		78
14		78		78
15	1,931	78	8	2,001

A decision to buy is indicated only for buildings of high and average flexibility. Apparently marginal results are partly the result of the notional one square foot building size. In Section 4 below a buy/sell decision for one of the 125 buildings in the City office sample is attempted using this model: this produces a realistic scale of results and confirms the importance of flexibility.

4. Applications

Three applications of this model are now to be illustrated. These are:

i a simple sensitivity test to explore the importance of depreciation as an input variable;

ii a buy/sell analysis at the individual property level, using a property derived from the City office sample; and

iii a buy/sell analysis at the property sector level, comparing refurbished and original buildings.

The sensitivity of return to depreciation

It is very difficult to undertake a controlled test of the sensitivity of return to depreciation, because depreciation is manifested in several inputs: rent, yield, expenditure and risk premium. A test of the individual impact of each input is possible, and is of some interest.

Building 002 again forms the basis of the test. The purpose is to vary individual inputs by 10% separately and to test the resulting impact on return, both NPV and IRR. Table 57 shows the results of this test.

Table 57 shows rental growth over each review to be the most important variable tested.   Given the multi-faceted nature of depreciation, it is, however, difficult to compare the relative impact of depreciation and rental growth by using these figures. A combined test is possible by comparing the impact of a 10% increase in all rental growth rates and a 10% increase in both rent and yield depreciation. Results are as shown in Table 58.

Table 57: Sensitivity of return (1)

Variable	Relative effect on NPV (%)	Relative effect on IRR (%)
Site value	0.00	0.00
Risk premium	-	1.49
Rental growth review 1	2.83	3.09
Rental growth review 2	2.26	2.45
Rental growth review 3	1.89	1.98
Dep'n in ERV to review 1	0.38	0.25
Dep'n in ERV to review 2	0.38	0.25
Dep'n in ERV to review 3	0.09	0.06
Dep'n in yield	0.75	0.50

Table 58: Sensitivity of return (2)

Variable	Relative effect on NPV (%)	Relative effect on IRR (%)
Rental growth	6.88	8.05
Depreciation	1.32	1.24

These figures show return to be 5 or 6 times as sensitive to input rental growth as to input depreciation rates. These are average depreciation values. Note, however, the impact of a change in building flexibility, shown comparatively in Table 59. The effects of an increase in grade from 2 to 3 and a reduction from 2 to 1 are both shown to take account of skewness.

While this is not a strictly comparable test, it can clearly be argued that the perceived importance of building quality suggested in this thesis and confirmed in Chapters 6 and 7 is further emphasised by this table.

Table 59: Sensitivity of return (3)

Variable		Relative effect on NPV (%)	Relative effect on IRR (%)
Rental growth		6.88	8.05
Depreciation		1.32	1.24
Flexibility	(increase)	4.43	7.92
	(decrease)	9.61	11.88

As Table 56 showed, building flexibility has a large impact on the outputs of the model, and can easily change a buy decision into a sell, and vice versa. Changes in input depreciation rate, on the other hand, are much less likely to change a decision on the evidence of these particular relationships.

The buy/sell decision

The major intended use of the model is to identify under-priced and over-priced investments. This can be attempted at the individual property level to aid purchase/sell/hold decisions for the individual investment: see below. Investment analysis of this type may also be carried out across sectors to aid investment strategy decisions. Examples of this type of analysis may include comparing offices against industrials, London offices against provincial offices, City offices against West End offices, and so on, in order to identify incorrectly priced sectors and to prompt action at the individual property level. The choice between original buildings and refurbishments within the central City office sample (see Chapter 5) is examined later in this sub-section for the purposes of illustration.

Individual property analysis

The model may be used to help in a decision to buy or reject an offered property investment or, alternatively, to sell or hold an investment which forms part of the current portfolio. For illustration, it is to be assumed that one of the 125 City office properties which formed the sample analysed in Chapter 6 is to be considered for purchase.

The building was fully refurbished 4 years ago and is wholly average in respect of its building qualities: scores of 3 out of a maximum of 5 were awarded in the appraisal process for all four building qualities (configuration, internal specification, external appearance and deterioration). The input variables have the values shown below. The building size is 100,000 square feet.

1. Property reference: 006
2. Price: £69.09m (£690.09 per square foot)
3. Estimated rental value: £3.625m per annum
    (£36.25 per square foot)
4. Site value (estimated): £40m
5. Building flexibility: see below
6. Risk free rate: 9%
7. Risk premium: 1.5%
8. Rental growth at review 1, review 2 and review 3:
    8%, 8% and 8% *
9. Estimated rental value at review 1, review 2, and
    review 3: see below
10. Resale capitalisation rate: see below
11. Rent review fee: 7%
12. Expenditure required: nil

* Prime rents grew in the City area by 10.37% per annum over the period 1980 to 1986 (see Chapter 6). A reduced estimate of constant future growth of 8% per annum reflects the longer term forecast.

Building flexibility

Building flexibility is assessed using the model described in Section 2 above. This flexibility model requires answers to the following questions.

1. *Is the floor layout capable of flexible use?*
   The configuration score was disaggregated into separate scores for floor layout and floor-to-ceiling height. The score for floor layout was 4. This is a direct input into the model.

2. *Is the floor-to-ceiling height generous?*
   The score was 2. Again, this can be used directly.

3. *Can the services be easily upgraded?*
   The original score for internal specification was 3, which was upgraded to 5 when the building was reappraised as if refurbished (see Chapter 6, Section 2). This suggests excellent flexibility in this respect: hence a score of 5 is used.

4. *Are the interior fittings easily changed?*
For the same reason a score of 5 is used.

5. *Are the entrance hall and common areas capable of improvement?*
The original score of 3 is upgraded to 5 in the reappraisal. This again suggests excellent flexibility and a score of 5 is used.

6. *Is the external appearance capable of cost-effective alteration?*
For the reasons stated at 5 above, a high score is suggested. However, it was noted during the reappraisal process that re-cladding would not be possible. A score of 4 is therefore used.

7. *Is potential building deterioration likely to be curable?*
A score of 3 is upgraded by the notional refurbishment to 5. This suggests wholly curable deterioration, so that a score of 5 is used.

The total weighted score is 4.40. The building is therefore classified by the model clearly as of *high flexibility* (range 3.34 to 5.00).

Estimated rental value at review 1, review 2 and review 3

Estimated rental value at review 1, review 2, and review 3 can be estimated using the cross-section analysis in two ways:

  i   using the regression equation developed in Chapter 6 which explains rental value for a given age as a predictive model; or
  ii using the index of rents provided in Chapter 6.

Use of a *regression equation* has some advantages. It is more flexible: rental value at any age will be predicted. It also smooths out any extreme values at any point which may be thrown up by inconsistent data. Its operation is illustrated in the following text.

The equation (for all properties) is:
Depreciation (£) = 4.81 + 0.324 age

For property 006, the predicted rental value for a building aged 4 years would be as follows:

Depreciation (£) = 4.81 + (0.324*4) = 4.81 + 1.30 = £6.11
ERV = prime rent – £6.11 = £40.25 – £6.11 = £34.14

The advantages of using the regression basis summarised above are reduced by the usual problems encountered in using an explanatory model for prediction, one of which is the potentially inaccurate prediction of current ERV. For example, while the predicted rent of £34.14 is close to the actual value of £34, a new property whose ERV *could* be £40.25 would have a predicted value of £40.25 – £4.81 (= £35.44) using this equation.

In this case there is also a minor problem with the *index method* in that the rent indices presented in Tables 25, 26 and 27 show average rental values at points which do not coincide with the review dates. Approximations may be made, however, as the differences are small. The overriding advantages are simplicity and accurate non-linear forecasts which truly reflect the available data. For these reasons, the index method is preferred and illustrated from here on.

The index method is used as follows.   The rental value of refurbishments was found to be £34.24 at age 2.05, £30.50 at age 6.28, £30.30 at age 11.08 and £26.97 at age 15.50. These values may be used as proxies for values at ages 4, 9, 14 and 19 with some adjustment. The estimated rental value of the subject building (£36.25 at age 4) compares with an average value of £34.24 at age 2.05. In order that this value might represent the actual age of 4, the appropriate adjustment is 1.059. Adjusted values for reviews 1, 2 and 3 are £32.30, £32.09 and £28.56 per square foot respectively.

Resale capitalisation rate

The same (index) method is used for yields. In Chapter 6 the average yield for refurbishments aged 2.05 years is shown to be 5.095%. The actual yield of property 006, age 4, is 5.25%. The appropriate adjustment is 1.03. The average yield at age 15.5 (used as a proxy for the end of a 15-year holding period, which should be year 19) is 5.923%; adjusted, this becomes 6.103%. Values are therefore as shown below.

```
Rent at review 1 (age 9):   = £3,230,000
Rent at review 2 (age 14):  = £3,209,000
Rent at review 3 (age 19):  = £2,856,000
Yield at review 3 (age 19): = 6.103%
```

Feeding these values into the model produces the following analysis (a full printout is reproduced as Appendix B).

ANALYSIS	
Target rate (%)	10.25
NPV (£)	5,076,530
IRR (%)	10.94
Decision:	buy

A purchase is advised. If the building were judged to be of low or even average flexibility a decision not to buy would result. (Results are IRRs of 8.97% and 10.13% respectively.) The importance of building flexibility is thereby illustrated. Given that it is possible that the market for investments of this type may be subject to some inefficiency and that the potential resistance to depreciation which is provided by buildings of particular quality and flexibility may not be fully taken into account in market price, the distinction between high, average and low flexibility buildings is, as the sensitivity analysis suggests, apparently crucial to the decision.

Property sector analysis

A comparison between sectors of the property market will identify purchase or sale candidates due to a systematic under- or over-pricing of property types. At any one time, a decision model such as this may suggest, for example, that offices are better buys than shops, or that City offices are better buys than provincial offices. The use of the model in the analysis of property sectors is illustrated by comparing original and refurbished City office buildings.

It was suggested in Chapter 5 that the performance of refurbishments may be distinguishable from that of original buildings. The decision model was therefore used to produce a generalised comparison between these sectors. It was employed to compare the anticipated returns on newly refurbished and original new central City office buildings given cross-section estimates of rent and yield depreciation. Average rental values at years 0, 5, 10 and 15 and average yields at years 0 and 15 were used to build simple cash flow estimates.

Property-specific inputs are as shown in Table 60 below; general inputs are as for property 006, analysed in Appendix B. Each analysis is carried out on the basis that properties are of average flexibility, and the risk premium is constant in the calculation of NPV.

If 1986 patterns are expected to be repeated in the future, Table 60 indicates a possible market inefficiency and confirms the suggestion that refurbishments may be less attractive. Note, however, that this analysis does not penalise refurbishments for reduced flexibility and increased risk: these factors are kept constant in the analysis. A reduction in the building flexibility score for refurbishments by one grade to reflect their reduced flexiblity (see Chapter 5) would reduce the IRR further by nearly 2% to 8.06%. An increase in the risk premium would reduce NPV even more.

Table 60: A comparative analysis of original buildings and refurbishments

Type of property	Price (£) at review 0	Rental value (£) at review				Yield (%) at reveiw		NPV (£)	IRR (%)
		0	1	2	3	0	3		
Original	779	36.76	36.73	35.36	34.05	4.716	5.457	23	10.78
Refurb'd	672	34.24	30.50	30.30	26.97	5.095	5.923	(34)	9.99

It is therefore reasonable to suggest that the City office market at 1986 failed to correctly distinguish original buildings and refurbishments on the evidence of the cross-section analysis. Further, either or both sectors were, on average, mispriced – original buildings were too cheap, and/or refurbishments were too expensive.

5. Conclusions

A decision model which incorporates depreciation as a variable is inevitably complex. The model presented herein is intended to be comprehensive and consequently may be more complex than is strictly necessary. Analysts would no doubt find it a straightforward matter to simplify the model, for example to ignore site value as a safety net; to assume one growth rate, and even one depreciation rate; and to ignore pre-set judgements over flexibility and refurbishment costs and to enter all variables flowing from these manually. As these adjustments are made, the model's flexibility increases at the cost of losing its empirical basis. This may be perfectly correct if the central City office market in mid-1986 is thought not to be a general guide to the future of the sub-market under consideration. Nonetheless, the model in its developed forms demonstrates several useful facts.

Firstly, the return on individual property investments is highly sensitive to building flexibility and hence to depreciation, which was shown to be at least as important as the most important of the other variables, rental growth. In an example derived from the sample, it was shown that a building of high flexibility was a profitable purchase; a building similar in other respects but of average or low flexibility was not.

Secondly, there may be price inefficiencies within sectors of the property market caused by lack of knowledge about depreciation. In this chapter it has been shown that participators in the central City office market failed to correctly price refurbishments and original buildings relative to each other: original buildings appear to be relatively cheap as they produced higher projected returns over the 15-year holding period. Yields are higher for refurbishments, but not high enough in relation to original buildings.

Finally, it may be generally concluded that in any particular case market pricing may be inaccurate due to a failure to reflect building flexibility and hence resistance to depreciation correctly. Higher returns may be made by market participants with a superior knowledge of the impact of depreciation.

Chapter 9

Conclusions and further work

1. Introduction

The early 1980's saw a rapid development of interest in property depreciation and obsolescence. Observation of the increasingly regular need for the refurbishment of office and industrial buildings, coupled with growing dissatisfaction with the quality of 1960's office buildings, led to falls in real value (and even nominal value in some years) in both sectors of the market (see Chapters 1 and 3). At the same time there evolved a realisation that conventional methods of property investment valuation and analysis were not equipped to deal with this phenomenon, together with a suspicion that the market price of depreciation-prone property investments was being set in an inefficient market. Characterising this market was a lack of knowledge about the sensitivity of property investment types to obsolescence and depreciation; there was also confusion regarding the relationship between these terms.

The CALUS study, undertaken in 1984-5 and published in 1986, was the first major attempt to address many of these issues and was specific in its identification of two objectives of necessary further research. These were: to expose the forces behind depreciation; and to set up analytical models which enable decision makers to make due allowance for it. This book has described research which set out to address both issues.

The context within which property investment decisions are made and a framework for a decision model are explained in Chapters 1 and 2. The framework is further developed to become capable of explicit analysis of depreciation in Chapter 8. The decision model relies upon the development of a classification model in Chapter 4.

The forces behind depreciation are identified by a process which incorporates a literature review described in Chapter 3 and the implications of Chapters 1 and 2, and which culminates in Chapter 4's classification model. It is the purpose of Chapters 5, 6 and 7 to describe the establishment and results of empirical research which measures the importance of these forces, which can then be accurately taken into account in the decision model developed in Chapter 8.

The underlying hypothesis of this research is to the effect that a model which classifies the causes of depreciation provides a superior explanation of depreciation to one which relates depreciation rate to age alone. The main empirical test of this is a study of central City of London office buildings in which estimates of rental value, yield and capital value are tested against age and quantitative estimates of building quality. Both statistical and hierarchical approaches are used in regression-based analyses of results. A subsidiary study of industrial property was undertaken for the purposes of comparison and comprehensiveness.

Conclusions can be summarised in three main sets. Firstly, the major hypothesis is considered in Sections 2 and 3 of this chapter, which relate depreciation to age and building quality respectively. Secondly, by-products of the empirical studies are examined in Sections 4 and 5 which deal, respectively, with the relative importance of curable and incurable depreciation and with the changing pace of depreciation between property types and over time. Thirdly, the investment implications are summarised in Section 6, which deals with the impact of depreciation on performance, and by setting empirical results against the framework of analytical decision models revisits the implications of the study for pricing efficiency in the City office market. Certain other hypotheses accumulated during the course of this research are listed in a final section, which sets out an agenda for further work.

Reservations must be stated. It may be that these conclusions are not unqualifiedly generalisable. Results may not be representative of other locations or other points in time, or of other market sectors.

Before proceeding to summarise these conclusions and suggestions for further work, it is useful to re-state definitions. As suggested in the beginning paragraph of this chapter, there has been confusion regarding the relationship and perceived interchangeability of the terms depreciation and obsolescence. The following definitions form the basis of the research.

Depreciation is a loss in the value of a property investment. Because depreciation is a problem even in times of increasing values, it should be more fully defined as a loss in the real value of a property investment. Because the grant of valuable planning permissions can disguise depreciation, a complete definition for this research is a **loss in the real existing use value of a property investment**.

Obsolescence, on the other hand, is one of the causes of depreciation. It is a **decline in utility not directly related to physical usage or the passage of time**. By contrast, other causes of building depreciation – physical deterioration being the main one – fall outside the definition of obsolescence. Obsolescence results from changes which are extraneous to the building.

There are three fundamental qualities of a building which are affected differently by physical deterioration and building obsolescence as the twin causes of building depreciation. These are the external appearance, which suffers from both; the internal specification, which suffers from both; and the configuration of the building, which can suffer only from obsolescence.

2. Depreciation and age

The key to improved decision-making is not a complex decision model but sound estimates of future rental values and resale capitalisation rates. This requires an ability to forecast. However, the nature of obsolescence is that it is extremely difficult to predict by fundamental analysis. Current patterns of depreciation, suitably adjusted, may therefore present the best possible guide to the future for the average building within a given sector.

For City offices, the rate of depreciation as a building ages was found to be around 0.92% per annum in rental value (Table 25) over a range of mean ages of 1.94 to 34.44 years. This is much less than the CALUS value of around 3% per annum over 20 years for all office buildings. (The value for the first 20 years in this research can only be estimated, but is around 0.75% per annum).

In capital value terms, the annual average rate of depreciation is 1.22% over years 1.94 to 34.44, leaving the average building representing around 60% of its new value at age 34.44 (compare the CALUS result of 55% of *rental* value at age 20).

For industrials, the annual reduction in rental value as buildings aged was again less than the CALUS estimate of around 3%, being around 0.65% over 20 years and 0.5% over 40 years.

These average figures disguise the significant variation from the straight line pattern of depreciation suggested in the CALUS work.

3. Depreciation and building quality

The major hypothesis of this research was clearly proven in the main empirical study of City offices. Building quality is a better explanation of depreciation than is age. Given that all four measured building qualities were individually more highly correlated with rental value and capital value than was age, it is naturally the case that in combination they become greatly superior. The general hypothesis was found to be true for both offices and industrials.

For offices, obsolescence was clearly much more important than physical deterioration as a cause of depreciation. Of the obsolescence factors, internal specification is most important to both occupiers and investors and hence as an explanation of depreciation in capital values. This appears to be primarily a function of the provision of services.

For industrials, physical deterioration is a significant factor in creating depreciation in rental value.

4. Curable and incurable depreciation

There is a fundamental difference between curable and incurable depreciation. The former may require an investor to make a provision for refurbishment at a lease end, but is largely dealt with by occupiers under the terms of the standard lease. The latter impacts directly on the investor, and creates a less flexible and therefore more risky investment.

Of the two categories, incurable depreciation is marginally more important for offices, but is overwhelmingly more important for industrials. This has ramifications for the relative risks of the two sectors.

For offices, curable depreciation is primarily a function of internal specification, especially services, while incurable depreciation is very closely identified with configuration, especially the plan layout of the building. The key to minimisation of the impact of incurable depreciation is building flexibility, which is driven primarily by the quality of the floor layout, the ability to change the impact of the entrance hall and the ability to replace internal services.

5. The pace of depreciation

There is evidence of a considerable acceleration of the pace of depreciation in industrial property over the period of the very late 1970's through to the early 1980's. This evidence is subject to some doubt as a result of the impact of the advent of *hi-tech* property upon that market but is sufficient to make an assertion. The critical period of acceleration appears to have been 1979 to 1986.

For offices, no evidence of the accelerating pace of depreciation was examined. A comparison of the average depreciation rates for offices and industrials is, however, instructive.   The pace of depreciation has been 3 to 4 times as fast over the period 1979 to 1986 for industrials than it has for offices. Secondly, refurbished office buildings have shown a faster pace of depreciation than original office buildings (see Table 60, and Baum, 1989a).

6. The impact of depreciation and flexibility on pricing and performance

Building quality is greatly superior to age as an explanation of depreciation. The prediction of depreciation depends, however, upon a prediction of the future incidence of obsolescence, which is very difficult. Buildings should therefore be preferred if they are <u>flexible</u> in terms of configuration, internal specification and external appearance.

Building flexibility is the key to reducing the importance of incurable depreciation and hence to reducing the risk of property investment. The return on an investment is also likely to be sensitive to the flexibility of the building.

It may be generally concluded that in any particular market sector pricing may be inaccurate due to an inefficiency caused by a failure to reflect building flexibility and hence resistance to depreciation correctly. A more attractive risk/return ratio may be enjoyed by market participants with a superior knowledge of the impact of depreciation. It is not enough to relate depreciation simply to age; while the average building may depreciate at an average rate, the investor will be rewarded by an ability to select investments which are of above-average resistance to depreciation. This depends vitally upon building quality, and focuses particularly upon building flexibility.

Property investment decision-makers require explicit models for the analysis of opportunities which make an estimate of likely depreciation in rent and yield but which additionally acknowledge depreciation as a risky variable. The introduction of depreciation, which has been shown not to follow a straight line pattern, into an investment analysis produces variations in return according to the choice of holding period. The purchase of a new building, for example, may produce higher returns than the purchase of an old building due to market inefficiency and the irregular depreciation patterns described in Section 2 above, without taking on higher risk.

A comparison may be drawn between the pricing of industrials and offices. Given that the former are much more prone to incurable depreciation, they are more risky. This justifies a higher risk premium and a higher target rate. It may explain to some extent the market differential of the 1980's, when average industrial yields exceeded average office yields by between one and four percentage points (see Table 5, Chapter 3).

A comparison may also be made between refurbished and original office buildings. The former depreciate more rapidly and are riskier (Baum, 1989a and Table 60). They deserve to attract a higher yield. There may be price inefficiencies which are capable of exploitation: in this research it was shown that participants in the central City office market failed to correctly price refurbishments and original office buildings relative to each other. Original buildings appear to have been relatively cheap. This tempts conclusions regarding the inability of investors to predict depreciation in rental values.

7. Further work

In the course of research, several hypotheses were suggested by observation but were not formally tested. They may form natural platforms for further research beyond that question.

Further development of this work is possible in four main areas.

1. It would be extremely useful to expand the research method to cover other sub-sectors of the property market, to include (for example) shopping centres, West End and provincial offices, other industrial sub-markets and even, perhaps, residential property. It would also be useful to repeat the City office study at (say) 5-yearly intervals, or to track the performance of the data set year by year. This would add greatly to the strength of the conclusions regarding the pace of, and patterns of, depreciation over time.

2. In an inefficient market which fails to clearly recognise the impact of depreciation on rent and especially yield, and in which annual valuations are the most important factor in the measurement of the investment performance of property, there is a strong chance that accumulated depreciation and its effect on performance may be disguised by the artificiality of valuations and rent reviews. Given the general growth in the depreciation rate over the holding period of a property investment, the effect of a building being tenanted is to ensure a rapid drop in value at the lease end. Should performance

measurement techniques be amended to allow for accumulated depreciation? Should this be dealt with by more explicit valuation techniques?

3. Depreciation may be predicted more accurately by combining judgements of flexibility, deterioration and the age variable in a multiple regression equation. It would be possible to use the data contained herein to test this hypothesis and to use the results in a revised decision model.

4. The return and risk of, and the correlation between, asset classes within a property portfolio will determine portfolio risk and return, and informed mixes will optimise the risk-return trade-off. In a market which is increasingly embracing modern portfolio theory as a guide to portfolio construction, efficient diversification is sought. It is generally driven by recognition of market segmentation by sector and region. Other property attributes may, however, be more fruitful as a means of efficient diversification. Is the level of resistance to depreciation a factor which will – or should – govern the future diversification of property portfolios?

Appendix A

Glossary of definitions

1. *Depreciation:* a loss in the real existing use value of a property investment.

2. *Tenure factors:* encumbrances and restrictions upon a property investment resulting from leases, tenancies or statutes which contribute to depreciation.

3. *Property factors:* factors which affect the rate of depreciation and which are indendent of tenure factors, relating to the quality of the site or the building.

4. *Property-specific depreciation:* depreciation resulting from property factors only.

5. *Site value change:* a change in the value of the site and not the building constructed upon it.

6. *Building depreciation:* depreciation in the notional value of the building and not the site upon which it stands.

7. *Environmental obsolescence:* the diminished utility and hence value of a property due to negative environmental forces in the surrounding area, such as detrimental neighbouring uses or unattractive neighbouring buildings.

8. *Supply and demand factors:* factors which may affect the value of a site related to the general level of economic activity, the general level of activity in the property market, the level of activity in the particular sector of the property market under consideration and local activity in that sub-market.

9. *Physical deterioration:* deterioration of the physical fabric of the exterior, interior and structure of the building and its services as a function of physical usage and the action of the elements.

10. *Building obsolescence:* a decline in the utility of a building that is not caused directly by physical usage, the action of the elements or the passage of time. Building obsolescence results from change which is extraneous to the building in question, such as altered market perceptions about design quality.

11. *Aesthetic obsolescence:* obsolescence resulting from an unfashionable style or design.

12. *Functional obsolescence:* obsolescence caused by changes in occupiers' building performance requirements, resulting from technological change, increases in standards or the introduction of new building products.

13. *External appearance:* the visual/psychological impact created by the exterior form of a building, its main entrance hall and its common areas.

14. *Internal specification:* the quality, quantity and state of repair of finishes, fittings and services within the building.

15. *Configuration:* the arrangement of the accommodation in terms of both plan layout and floor-to-ceiling height and its impact upon flexibility of use.

16. *External design:* the visual/psychological impact created by the exterior form of a building.

17. *Impact of entrance:* the visual/psychological impact created by the main entrance (interior and exterior) to the building, and all common areas in that building.

18. *Internal finishes:* the quality, style, utility and state of repair of the internal finishes and fittings of the building.

19. *Services:* the quality, style, state of repair, specification and efficiency of mechanical and electrical services to the building.

20. *Floor-to-ceiling heights:* the slab-to-slab heights as they affect the ability of the building to accept technology above each lower slab and/or below each upper slab.

21. *Floor layout etc:* the plan shape of the building and the arrangement of cores, window modules, natural lighting and columns and so on, with particular reference to the effect upon the flexibility of use of the accommodation.

22. *Curable depreciation:* such depreciation which costs a lesser or equal amount to cure than the value that will be added to the property as a result.

23. *Incurable depreciation:* such depreciation which costs a greater amount to cure than the value that will be added to the property as a result.

Appendix B

Analysis of property 006

Input variables		
Property reference		006
Price	(£)	69,090,000
ERV	(£)	3,625,000
Site value	(£)	40,000,000
Building flexibility		3
Risk free rate	(%)	9.00
Risk premium	(%)	1.50
Rental growth review 1 pa	(%)	8.00
Rental growth review 2 pa	(%)	8.00
Rental growth review 3 pa	(%)	8.00
Current ERV review 1	(£)	3,230,000
Current ERV review 2	(£)	3,209,000
Current ERV review 3	(£)	2,856,000
Current capitalisation rate	(%)	5.247
Resale capitalisation rate	(%)	6.103
Rent review fee	(%)	7.00
Expenditure: amount		0
Expenditure: year		0

Flexibility adjustments			
Building flexibility	Low (1)	Average (2)	High(3)
Current ERV at review 1 (£)	2,835,000	3,230,000	3,427,500
Current ERV at review 2 (£)	2,793,000	3,209,000	3,417,000
Current ERV at review 3 (£)	2,087,000	2,856,000	3,240,000
Resale capitalisation rate (%)	7.53	6.10	5.53
Risk premium (%)	1.75	1.50	1.25

Projections		
Projected ERV dep'n pa, review 1	(%)	1.07
Projected ERV dep'n pa, review 2	(%)	0.06
Projected ERV dep'n pa, review 3	(%)	1.01
Projected average SL ERV dep'n pa	(%)	0.67
Projected average CV dep'n pa	(%)	1.40
Projected ERV, review 1	(£)	5,036,122
Projected ERV, review 2	(£)	7,377,047
Projected ERV, review 3	(£)	10,279,414
Projected site value	(£)	126,886,765
Projected net resale	(£)	168,432,148
Projected realisation	(£)	168,432,148

Analysis		
Target rate	(%)	10.25
NPV	(£)	5,076,530
IRR	(%)	10.94

Cash flow statement				
Year	Capital (£)	Income (£)	Outflow (£)	Net Cash (£)
1	(69,090,000)	3,625,000		(69,090,000)
2		3,625,000		3,625,000
3		3,625,000		3,625,000
4		3,625,000		3,625,000
5		3,625,000	352,529	3,272,471
6		5,036,122		5,036,122
7		5,036,122		5,036,122
8		5,036,122		5,036,122
9		5,036,122		5,036,122
10		5,036,122	516,393	4,519,729
11		7,377,047		7,377,047
12		7,377,047		7,377,047
13		7,377,047		7,377,047
14		7,377,047		7,377,047
15	168,432,148	7,377,047	719,559	175,089,636

References

Chapter 1

Baum, A E (1989b) <u>A Critical Examination of the Measurement of Property Investment Risk</u>, Department of Land Economy Discussion Paper No 22, University of Cambridge

Baum, A E and Crosby, F N (1988) <u>Property Investment Appraisal</u>, London: Routledge

Branch, B (1985) <u>Investments: A Practical Approach</u>, Chicago: Longman

Brigham, E (1985) <u>Financial Management: Theory and Practice</u> (4e), Chicago: Dryden

Brown, G (1985) <u>An Empirical Analysis of Risk and Return in the UK Commercial Property Market</u>, unpublished PhD thesis, University of Reading

Crosby, N (1985) <u>The Application of Equated Yield and Real Value Approaches to the Market Valuation of Commercial Property Investments</u>, unpublished PhD thesis, University of Reading

Fraser, W (1984) <u>Principles of Property Investment and Pricing</u>, London: Macmillan

Fraser, W (1985) <u>Gilt Yields and Property's Target Return</u>, Estates Gazette 273: 1291

Gitman, L and Joehnk, M (1984) <u>Fundamentals of Investing</u>, New York: Harper and Row

Greer, G and Farrell, M (1979) <u>The Real Estate Investment Decision</u>, Lexington: Lexington Books

Hargitay, S (1983) <u>A Systematic Approach to the Analysis of the Property Portfolio</u>, unpublished PhD thesis, University of Reading

Investors Chronicle Hillier Parker (1988) <u>Average Yields</u>, London: ICHP

Investors Chronicle Hillier Parker (1988) <u>Rent Index</u>, London: ICHP

Jacob, N and Pettit, B (1984) <u>Investments</u>, Irwin: Homewood

McIntosh, A P J and Sykes, S G (1985) <u>A Guide to Institutional Property Investment</u>, London: Macmillan

Markowitz, H (1959) <u>Portfolio Selection – Efficient Diversification of Investments</u>, New Haven: Yale University Press

Marriott, O (1967) The Property Boom, London: Pan

Reilly, F (1985) Investment Analysis and Portfolio Management, Chicago: Dryden

Rose, J (1985) The Dynamics of Urban Property Development, London: Spon

Salway, F W (1986) Depreciation of Commercial Property, Reading: CALUS

Sharpe, W (1964) Capital Asset Prices: A Theory of Market Equilibrium Under Conditions of Risk, Journal of Finance, September, p.425

Ward, C (1979) The Methods of Incorporating Risk in the Analysis of Commercial Property Investment, unpublished PhD thesis, University of Reading

Chapter 2

Baum, A E and Crosby, N (1988) Property Investment Appraisal, London: Routledge

Baum, A E (1987) Risk-Explicit Appraisal: a Sliced-Income Approach, Journal of Valuation, 5: 250

Baum, A E (1984) The Valuation of Reversionary Freeholds: a Review, Journal of Valuation, 3: 53

Baum, A E and Yu, S M (1985) The Valuation of Leaseholds: a Review, Journal of Valuation, 3: 157 and 3: 230

Baum, A E and Butler, D (1986) The Valuation of Short Leasehold Investments, Journal of Valuation, 4: 342

Brealey, E and Myers, S (1984) Principles of Corporate Finance, New York: McGraw Hill

Brigham, E (1985) Financial Management: Theory and Practice (4e), Chicago: Dryden

Brown, G (1985) An Empirical Analysis of Risk and Return in the UK Commercial Property Market, unpublished PhD thesis, University of Reading

Byrne, P and Cadman, D (1984) Risk, Uncertainty and Decision-Making in Property Development, London: Spon

Crosby, N (1985) The Application of Equated Yield and Real Value Approaches to the Market Valuation of Commercial Property Investments, unpublished PhD thesis, University of Reading

Debenham, Tewson and Chinnocks, (1985) Obsolescence: its Effect on the Valuation of Property Investments, London: Debenham, Tewson and Chinnocks

Field, B and MacGregor, B D (1987) Forecasting Techniques for Urban and Regional Planning, London: Hutchinson

Fisher, I (1930) The Theory of Interest, Philadelphia: Porcupine Press

Greenwell, W and Co (1976) A Call for New Valuation Methods, Estates Gazette 238: 481

Greer, G and Farrell, M (1984) Investment Analysis for Real Estate Decisions, Chicago: Dryden

Jaffe, A (1977) Is There a "New" Internal Rate of Return Literature?, American Real Estate and Urban Economics Association Journal, 5: 482

Korpacz, P and Roth, M (1983), Changing Emphasis in Appraisal Techniques: the Transition to Discounted Cash Flow, Journal of Valuation, 2: 19

Marshall, P (1976) Equated Yield Analysis, Estates Gazette,239: 493

Mason, R (1986) The Appraisal of Shop Investments, Journal of Valuation, 5: 147

Newell, M (1986) The Rate of Return as a Measure of Performance, Journal of Valuation, 4: 130

Reilly, F (1985) Investment Analysis and Portfolio Management, Chicago: Dryden

Robinson, J (1986) After Tax Cash Flow Analysis, Journal of Valuation, 5: 18

Robinson, J (1985) Property Investment Analysis by Lotus 1-2-3, Journal of Valuation, 4: 92

Sykes, S (1981) Property Valuation: A Rational Model, The Investment Analyst, 61: 20

Sykes, S and McIntosh, A (1982) Towards a Standard Property Income Valuation Model: Rationalisation or Stagnation? Journal of Valuation, 1: 117

Trott, A (1980) Property Valuation Methods: Interim Report, London: Polytechnic of the South Bank/RICS

Chapter 3

Accounting Standards Committee (1987) Statement of Standard Accounting Practice 12, London: ASC

Accounting Standards Committee (1987) Statement of Standard Accounting Practice 19, London: ASC

Armstrong, J H (1903) An Address to the Northern Institute of Chartered Accountants, The Accountant, August 8, p.1014

Baum, A E and Crosby, N (1988) Property Investment Appraisal, London: Routledge

Baum, A E (1989b) A Critical Examination of the Measurement of Property Investment Risk, Department of Land Economy Discussion Paper No 22, University of Cambridge

Blandon, P R and Ward, C W R (1978) Expectations in the Property Market, The Investment Analyst, 52:24

Bowie, N (1982) Depreciation: Who Hoodwinked Whom? Estates Gazette, 262:405

Bowie, N (1983a) The Depreciation of Buildings, Journal of Valuation, 2:5

Brown, G R (1970) Some Applications of Discounted Cash Flow Criteria to Problems of Architectural Design, unpublished MA thesis, University of Liverpool, School of Business Studies

Brown, G R (1986) A Note on the Analysis of Depreciation and Obsolescence, Journal of Valuation, 4:230

Cherry, A (1986) Valuing for Obsolescence, in The Workplace Revolution, London: Healey and Baker

Clarke, D (1986) The Trend Spotters with an Appreciation of Depreciation, Estates Times Supplement, Spring, p.62

Coates, M (1986) Core and Shell – The Space Revolution? Estates Gazette, 278:804

Coombes, J (1986) Landlord and Tenant Relationships and Management Implications, paper presented at CALUS Conference on Depreciation of Commercial Property, September 17

Coyne, C (1987) Unpublished report for Touche Ross, reported in *Financial Times*, April 8; paper presented at Building Industry Convention, Brighton, 1987

Debenham, Tewson and Chinnocks (1985) Obsolescence – Its Effect on the Valuation of Property Investments, London: Debenham Tewson and Chinnocks

Dew, M (1986) Investment Considerations, paper presented at CALUS Conference on Depreciation of Commercial Property, September 17

Duffy, F (1986) The City Revolution – Its Impact on Office Space, in The Workplace Revolution, London: Healey and Baker

Economic Advisory Group (1974) Office Rents in the City of London and their effects on Invisible Earnings, Committee on Invisible Exports, October

Edward Erdman Research (1987) Industrial Property Survey, London: Edward Erdman (June)

Ferguson, A (1987) Offices for Professionals, Estates Gazette,283:1148

Finn, M (1986), address to the 1986 Building Industry Convention, unpublished. Referred to in RICS Press Release, April 22

Fraser, W (1986) Property Yield Trends in a Fluctuating Economy, Journal of Valuation, 4:239

Hallett, M (1986) Valuation, Appraisal and Property Perfomance, paper presented at CALUS Conference on Depreciation of Commercial Property, September 17

Healey and Baker Research (1987) National Office Design Survey, London: Healey and Baker

Holmes, G and Sugden, A (1986) Interpreting Company Reports and Accounts (3e), London: Woodhead-Faulkner

Investors Chronicle Hillier Parker (1988) IHCP Property Market Indicators No 2, August

Pepper, D and Morgan, T (1986) The Key to Successful Office Planning, Investors Chronicle, November 7, p.32

Povall, S (1986) Building Design, paper presented at CALUS Conference on Depreciation of Commercial Property, September 17

Richard Ellis (1987) Quarterly Bulletin: Office Investment Outside Central London, London: Richard Ellis (April)

Royal Institution of Chartered Surveyors (1988) Guidance Notes on the Valuation of Assets, Asset Valuation Standards Committee

Salway, F (1986) Depreciation of Commercial Property, Reading: CALUS

Stringer, G (1986) How Long was the 1960's Building Meant to Last? paper presented to Henry Stewart Seventh Annual Structural Survey Conference, May 1

Sykes, S (1984a) Refurbishment and Future Rental Growth: the Implications, Estates Gazette, 272:1321

Sykes, S (1984b) Periodic Refurbishment and Rental Value Growth, Journal of Valuation, 3:32

Sykes, S (1986) Refurbishment and Expenditure – Just a Matter of Time, in The Workplace Revolution, London: Healey and Baker

Wilson, T (1985) Offices as an Investment, in Marber, P and Marber, P (Eds) Office Development, London: Estates Gazette

Chapter 4

Baxter, W T (1981) Depreciating Assets : An Introduction, London: Gee and Co for the Institute of Chartered Accountants of Scotland

Chapman, D H (1973) Technical Terms for Property People, London: Estates Gazette

Darlow, C (ed) (1983) Valuations and Development Appraisal, London: Estates Gazette

Davies, K (1978) Law of Compulsory Purchase and Compensation (3e), London: Butterworths

Fraser, W (1984) Principles of Property Investment and Pricing, London: Macmillan

Lichtenstein, P M (1983) An Introduction to Post-Keyensian and Marxian Theories of Value and Price, London: Macmillan

Salway, F (1986) Depreciation of Commercial Property, Reading: CALUS

Shenkel, W M (1984) Modern Real Estate Principles (3e), Plano: Business Publications

Wofford, L E (1983) Real Estate, (revised edition) New York: John Wiley

Wurtzebach, C H and Miles, M E (1984) Modern Real Estate (2e), New York: John Wiley

Chapter 5

Adams, A T and Baum, A E (1989) Property Securitisation: Premium or Discount? The Investment Analyst, January 31:38

Bowie, N (1982) Depreciation: Who Hoodwinked Whom? Estates Gazette, 262:405

Brown, G R (1986) A Note on the Analysis of Depreciation and Obsolescence, Journal of Valuation, 4:228

Jones Lang Wootton (1988) 50 Centres, London: Jones Lang Wootton

Richard Ellis (1986) The City Property Forecast, London: Richard Ellis

Salway, F (1986) Depreciation of Commercial Property, Reading: CALUS

RICS/Institute of Actuaries (quarterly), RICS/Actuaries Rent Index

Chapter 6

Baum, A E (1989a) An Analysis of Property Investment Depreciation and Obsolescence, Unpublished PhD thesis, University of Reading

Chapter 7

Bowie, N (1982) Depreciation: Who Hoodwinked Whom? Estates Gazette 262:405

Bowie, N (1982) Depreciation: Who Hoodwinked Whom? Estates Gazette 262:405

Edward Erdman Research (1987) Industrial Property Survey, London: Edward Erdman (June)

Evans, P and Plumb, C (1984) The Property Requirements of Knowledge-based Industries, Land Development Studies 1:131

Fraser, W (1986) Property Yield Trends in a Fluctuating Economy, Journal of Valuation, 4:239

Hall, P, Breheny, M, McQuaid, R and Hart, D (1987) Western Sunrise, London: Allen and Unwin

Hall, P and Markusen, A (1985) Silicon Landscapes, London: Allen and Unwin

Henneberry, J M (1984) Property for High-technology Industry, Land Development Studies, 1:145

Henneberry, J M (1986) Occupiers and their Use of Accommodation on Science Parks and High Technology Developments, Land Development Studies, 4:109

Hillier Parker (1987) Hi-tech Users, London: Hillier Parker

Hillier Parker (1988) Hi-tech Rent Index, London: Investors Chronicle Hillier Parker

Salway, F (1986) Depreciation of Commercial Property, Reading: CALUS

Waldy, E B D (1986) Business Parks, London: Fletcher King

Chapter 8

Baum, A E (1989a) An Analysis of Property Investment Depreciation and Obsolescence, Unpublished PhD thesis, University of Reading

Harker, N (1987) The Valuation of Modern Warehouses: Inflation and Depreciation Implications, Journal of Valuation, 5:138

Miles, J (1987) Depreciation and Valuation Accuracy, Journal of Valuation 5:125

Neter, J, Wasserman, W and Whitmore, G A (1982) Applied Statistics (2e), Boston: Allyn and Bacon

Salway, F (1986) Depreciation of Commercial Property: CALUS

Salway, F (1987) Building Depreciation and Property Appraisal Techniques, Journal of Valuation 5:118

Sykes, S (1984b) Periodic Refurbishment and Rental Value Growth, Journal of Valuation 5: 3:32

Chapter 9

Baum, A E (1989a) An Analysis of Property Investment Depreciation and Obsolescence, Unpublished PhD thesis, University of Reading

Further reading

Alberts, W W and Castania, R P (1982) The Impact of Changes in Tax Depreciation Rates on Holding Periods for Real Estate Investments, National Tax Journal 35(1): 43

American Institute of Real Estate Appraisers (1983) The Appraisal of Real Estate (6e), Chicago: AIREA

American Institute of Real Estate Appraisers (1984) The Dictionary of Real Estate Appraisal, Chicago: AIREA

Babcock, F M (1937) The Valuation of Real Estate, New York: McGraw Hill

Barratt, M (1986) Service Charges in Property: Shopping Centres, Reading: College of Estate Management

Baum, A E (1982) Depreciation: Some Alternative Approaches, The Valuer, 51(8) 168

Baum, A E (1983) Statutory Valuations, London: Routledge and Kegan Paul

Baxter, W T (1971) Depreciation, London: Sweet and Maxwell

Bonbright, J C (1937) The Valuation of Property, Volume I, New York: McGraw Hill

Bowie, N (1983b) The Reverse Yield Gap: How Deep and Wide Really Is It? Estates Gazette, 267:138

Bowie, N (1984) Learning to Take Account of Depreciation, Estates Times, June, p 13

BPP (1986) Interpretation of Financial Statements, London: BPP

Brannon, G M and Sunley, E M (1976) Recapture of Excess Tax Depreciation On Sale of Real Estate, National Tax Journal, 20(4):413

Brown, G R (1984) Assessing an All-Risks Yield, Estates Gazette, 269:700

Cannoday, R E and Sunderman, M A (1986) Estimation of Depreciation for Single-Family Appraisals, AREUEA Journal, 14(2): 255

Cantwell, R C (1988) Curable Functional Obsolescence: Deficiency Requiring Substitution or Modernisation, Appraisal Journal, July, p. 361

Cerf, A R (1983) Accounting for Real Estate Development, Accounting Review, 58(1): 205

Chow, G C (1960) Tests of Equality Between Sets of Coefficients in Two Linear Regressions, Econometrica, 28: 591

Clinch, G, (1983) Alternative Hypotheses Concerning Depreciation of Buildings, ABACUS, 19(2): 139

Copley, R E, and Clemons, M K (1983) Choosing the Right Depreciation Method: the Impact of Marginal Tax Brackets, Appraisal Journal, July, p. 355

Corgel, J B, and Goebel, P R (1979) Choosing Depreciable Lives: Weighing Gains Versus Risks, Real Estate Review, 9:80

Corgel, J B (1981) Useful Life, Component Depreciation, and the Economic Characteristics of Real Estate, Journal of Real Estate Taxation, 9(2): 125

Cowan, P (1965) Depreciation, Obsolescence and Ageing, Architects Journal, 141:1395

Crasswell, A T (1986) An Examination of Alternative Hypotheses Concerning Depreciation of Buildings, ABACUS, 22(1): 29

Cutsinger, S (1978) The Cost Approach May Produce the Lowest Valuation Estimate, Real Estate Appraiser, 44(1): 35

Debenham, Tewson and Chinnocks (1984) Office Rent and Rates, London: Debenham, Tewson and Chinnocks

Department of Trade and Industry (1986) The Rules Relating to Depreciation Charged on Evaluated Assets (consultative note), London: DTI

Derbes, M J (1982) Is the Cost Approach Obsolete? Appraisal Journal, 50(4):581

Eisen, D, (1984) Standard Analytical Techniques Give Inconsistent Answers About Commercial Property Depreciation, Real Estate Review, 14(3): 95

Englebrecht, T D (1977) Depreciation Recapture Under the Tax Reform Act, Real Estate Review, 7:18

Entreken, H C, and Kapplin, S D (1977) Proper Place and Purpose of the Cost Approach, Real Estate Appraiser, 43:5

Evans, A W (1985) Urban Economics, London: Macmillan

Fisher, J D and Leutz, G H, (1986) Tax Reform and the Value of Real Estate Income Property, AREUEA Journal 14(2): 287

Flanagan, R and Norman G (1983) Life Cycle Costing for Construction, London: RICS

Fraser, R R (1978) Depreciation and the Value of Real Estate, The Valuer (Australia), 25(4):276

Gilliland, C E (1979) Component Depreciation – the Appraiser's Role, Appraisal Journal, 48:78

Goldberg, L (1960) Concepts of Depreciation, Harston, Australia: Partridge and Co. Pty. Ltd.

Goodman, L, (1986) Depreciation Recapture Rules Can Create Problems for Real Estate Investors, Real Estate Law Journal, 15(1): 56

Greaves, M J (1985) The Determination of Residential Values: the Hierarchical and Statistical Approaches, Journal of Valuation, 3: 5

Greer, G and Farrell, M (1984) Investment Analysis for Real Estate Decisions, Chicago: Dryden

Hargreaves, R V (1983a) Some Computer Applications to the Replacement Cost Method of Valuation. Wellington: New Zealand Institute of Valuers (New Technology Committee publication no.2)

Hargreaves, R V (1983b) Further Computer Applications To the Valuation Process, Wellington: New Zealand Institute of Valuers (New Technology Committee publication no. 3)

Harris, D G, (1984) Real Property Depreciation and the Homeowner, Taxes 62(1): 54

Hartman, Donald J, and Shapiro, M B (1983) Depreciation: Incurable Functional Obsolescence and Sequence of Deductions, Appraisal Journal, 51(3):408

Hartman, Donald J (1977) Industrial Real Estate: Cost Approach with Caution, Appraisal Journal, 45(3):444

Hendershott, P H and Ling, D C (1984a) Prospective Changes in Tax Law and the Value of Depreciable Real Estate, AREUEA Journal, 12(3): 297

Hendershott, P H and Ling, D C (1984b) Trading and the Tax-Shelter Value of Depreciable Real Estate, National Tax Journal, 37(2): 213

Henley Management College (1985) A Study of the Cost of Office Premises in England, Henley: Henley Management College

Higgins, J W (1977) Maximising Depreciation Through Component Depreciation, Real Estate Appraiser, 42:52

Higgins, J W and Scribner, D (1976) Simple Formula for Switching Declining Balance to Straight-Line When Depreciating Real Property, Real Estate Appraiser, 42:36

Howell, R G and Renold, J (1970) Data on the Deterioration of Building Elements, London: Local Government Operational Research Unit (September)

Hutton, G H and Devonald, A D G (1973) Value in Building, London: Applied Science Publishers Ltd

Hyder, K L (1966) Depreciation, Obsolescence and Lack of Utility in Residential Property, The Valuer (Australia), 13(6): 293

Institute of Chartered Accountants in England and Wales (1981) Accounting for Investment Properties, (SSAP19), London: ICAEW

Institute of Chartered Accountants in England And Wales (1983) Accounting for Depreciation (exposure draft), London: ICAEW

Institute of Chartered Accountants in England and Wales (1987) Accounting for Depreciation (SSAP12), London: ICAEW

Jones Lang Wootton (1987) Obsolescence: its Impact on Property Performance, London: Jones Lang Wootton

Kanner, G (1978) Reproduction Less Depreciation: Real World Economics in the Courts, Appraisal Journal, 46(4):68

Kay, D B (1973) Valuation Research Papers, Western Australian Institute of Technology

Krasker, W S (1982) Building Depreciation: Which Method Pays Off? Harvard Business Review, 60(6):68

Larkin, D (1986) Big Bang: the Property Implications, Investors Chronicle, 7:32

Ling, D C (1984) The Valuation of Depreciable Real Estate, unpublished PhD thesis, Ohio State University

Ling, D C and Whinihan, M J (1985) Valuing Depreciable Real Estate: a New Methodology, AREUEA Journal, 13(2): 181

MacGregor, B D, Baum, A E, Adams, C, Fleming, S and Peterson, J (1984) Land Availability for Inner City Development, Department of Land Management, University of Reading

Mainly for Students (1986) Insurance and DRC Valuations, Estates Gazette, 278:228

Moreton, N and Tate, J (1986) House Pricing in the Older Housing Stock of Birmingham, Housing Review 35(3):85

Newman, R H (1949) A Critical Study in Depreciation, Digest of New Zealand Valuer, June

Nicoletti, M (1986) Obsolescence, Architectural Review, 143:412

Nobes, C (1979) The Reality of Property Depreciation, Accountancy, November, p.129

Nobes, C (1979) Property Depreciation: Now Let's be Realistic, Accountancy, December, p.50

Nobes, C (1985) Depreciation: Can a New Standard Clear the Way? Accountancy, March, p.110

North, L (1984) Propitious Use of the Cost Approach Cuts Variables, Estates Times, 752:10

Orchard-Lisle, P (1986) New Thinking in the Property Market, Investors Chronicle, 7:22

Patchin, P J (1979) How Depreciation Methods Conform to Actual Market Experience. Appraisal Journal, 48(4):503

Patient, M (1984) Depreciation on Revalued Fixed Assets, Accountancy, June, p.15

Pindyck, R S and Rubinfeld, D L (1981) Econometric Models and Economic Forecasts (2e), New York: McGraw Hill

Powell, J G (1977) Depreciation Under Current Cost Accounting, Estates Gazette, 283:1148

Powell, J G (1984) Valuation for Corporate Purposes: Asset Valuation, Journal of Valuation, 2:403

Ratcliff, R U (1968) Modern Real Estate Valuation, Ontario: Clintwood Printing

Ratcliff, R U (1972) Valuation for Real Estate Decisions, Democrat Press, 1972

Rayner, Michael (1981) Valuation of Property Assets for Which No Market Exists, Estates Gazette, 238:549

Richard Ellis and Hill Samuel Property Services Ltd, (1988) Property Investment Depreciation and Obsolescence, London: Richard Ellis and Hill Samuel Property Services Ltd.

Rose, M (1978) Property Companies Parry SSAP 12 on Depreciation, Accountancy, December, p.15

Royal Institution of Chartered Surveyors (1981) Guidance Notes on the Valuation of Assets (2e): Background paper no.6: Negative Values, London: RICS

Rutterford, J (1986) Introduction to Stock Exchange Investment, London: Macmillan.

Schneider, W J (1984) Straight Line and Accelerated Depreciation: an Analytical Approach, Industrial Development, May-June

Sharpe, W (1985) Investments (3e), New Jersey: Prentice

Speedy, S L (1974) Property Investment, Wellington: Butterworths

Speedy, S L (1983) Recent Problems in Capital Recovery (Depreciation) The Valuer, January, p. 440

Speedy, S L (1984) Valuation for Corporate Purposes: Current Cost Accounting Perspectives, Journal of Valuation, 2:420

Switzer, J F Q (1963) The Life of Buildings in an Expanding Economy, <u>Chartered Surveyor</u>, August, p.70

Thayer, R E (1983) Rethinking the Cost Approach to Valuation, <u>Appraisal Journal</u>, 51(2):278

Thomas, J J (1983) <u>An Introduction to Statistical Analysis for Economists</u> (2e), London: Wiedenfeld and Nicholson

Tidwell, V H (1977) Component Depreciation Can be a Cure for Excess Depreciation, <u>Taxes</u>, 55:116

Tucker, S F (1979) Real Estate Depreciation – Fresh Examination of the Basic Rules, <u>Journal of Real Estate Taxation</u> 6(2): 101

Various (1979) Accounting for Depreciation, <u>Chartered Surveyor</u>, 111(6) p. 205

Various (1986) <u>Refurbishments: a Key to Unlocking Profits</u>, unpublished Longman conference paper

Westwick, C A (1982) <u>Property Valuation and Accounts</u>, London: ICAEW

Williford, J S (1977) Selecting Useful Lives in Depreciation of Buildings, <u>Real Estate Review</u> 7(3): 31

Williford, J S (1978) There's a Right Way to Compute Depreciation, <u>Buildings</u>, October, p. 95

Yu, S M (1978) <u>Depreciation in Single Residential Property</u>, unpublished diploma dissertation, University of Auckland

Zangerle, J A (1927) <u>Principles of Real Estate Appraising</u>, Cleveland: Stanley McMichael Publishing Organization

Index